Dublindining

New Recipes from Dublin's Finest Chefs

Edited by PAUL RANKIN
Photographs by STEPHEN KEARNEY

BLACK & WHITE PUBLISHING

We have reproduced the recipes as supplied by the
chefs, according to their own individual cooking styles.
All recipes serve four, unless otherwise stated.

First published 2002
by Black & White Publishing Ltd,
99 Giles Street, Edinburgh EH6 6BZ

ISBN 1 902927 37 0

Introduction © Paul Rankin 2002
Recipes © The contributing establishments 2002
All photographs © Stephen Kearney

British Library Cataloguing in Publication data: a catalogue record for
this book is available from The British Library.

With grateful thanks to Orla Broderick for all her help and support with
this volume.

Copy editing by Patricia Marshall
Book design by Creative Link
Layout design by Janene Reid

Printed and bound in Spain by Bookprint, S.L., Barcelona

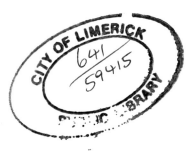

Contents

Introduction

BY PAUL RANKIN

Talented chefs, fine cooks, great craic, wonderful hospitality, Celtic spirit, raw energy, world class products . . . these are the elements that combine to make up the extraordinary variety and quality of *Dublin Dining*.

My, we have come such a long way in the last ten years. With the help of the Celtic Tiger economy we have been travelling more, eating more amazing foreign meals, experiencing new tastes and flavours. Our supermarkets are teeming with new kinds of produce, spices, condiments. Why, it seems like only yesterday that a good friend of mine asked me, 'Have you ever tasted garlic?'. Bookshops are full of exciting cook-books and magazines – we use them as bedtime reading, getting ideas for the weekend's dinner party. Some may comment on the number of cookery shows on television, but the networks would not show them if there wasn't the demand. We have fallen in love with food, and that is great news for the restaurant industry.

A dozen years ago it would have been said that Dublin had a handful of decent restaurants. Nowadays, all agree that we are spoilt for choice. This book is by no means an exhaustive list. There are plenty more out there, and I'm sure that I'll be buying a few pints and bottles of champagne for friends who wonder why they aren't in this beautiful book. I shall explain that there'll need to be a second volume, but until that time, this book is the ultimate celebration of Dublin restaurants.

One of my favourite pastimes bar none is visiting new cities and searching out fine food. I seem to have a knack for being able to 'judge a book by its cover', so to speak. Each good place gives out clues to the committed foodie, and I can spot those clues a mile away. The menu is usually the first, of course. How is it written? How regional is it? Does it seem authentic? Does it have the reek of real cooking, or is it formulaic? Other clues might be the glassware, cutlery, the type of coffee on offer, a bottle of olive oil on the sideboard, or discarded fresh artichoke leaves in a cardboard box . . . I'm never really sure exactly what I'm looking for, but I do love the game – and the results. Consider the menu at O'Connells in Ballsbridge. It proudly displays Frank Hederman's smoked fish on the menu. Frank's smoked seafood is so good it's famous abroad as well as here in Ireland. It's not cheap, of course, but it is local, quality produce – the chef's greatest asset – and it shows that a restaurant cares and is trying hard. Irish Angus beef at Shanahan's, now that sounds good. Conakilty black pudding at L'Ecrivain, Irish and proud of it. Blue lobster at Pearl Brasserie . . . mmm, that's local, the real McCoy, none of that tired Canadian stuff.

As you read through this book, you'll notice that every chef is absolutely passionate about the produce. Why? Because that is where good food starts, using the best local produce available. Lucky for all of us that Ireland has some of the very best produce in the world. Here are a few cookery tips from our chefs. John Dunne, of Avoca Café, says he relies on 'the freshest and highest quality seasonal ingredients, treated simply to show them off'. (Training under the likes of Raymond Blanc does, of course, add a distinct advantage.) At Cavistons, a Dublin institution, Peter Caviston knows what he is doing. 'Our menu is based around the day's catch so that it tastes as if it's just been brought in by the Irish fishing fleet . . . nothing fancy, nothing complicated, just simple, fresh food that speaks for itself.' This is just the sort of talk that I personally fall for every time. (By the way, it's a very big clue when you see a counter full of gleaming fresh fish at the front of the restaurant!)

One of the things that I love about Dublin restaurants is their spirit. Each has individuality, which I believe is a must. They all show a strong sense of who they are, what they do, and whom they do it for. And it's so inspiring to have brave restaurateurs like David Hui at China Sichuan. He took the step of opening an authentic Sichuan restaurant in 1986 when in Ireland very few would have known what a whole peppercorn was, let alone a Sichuan peppercorn. David says that he 'took the bull by the horns, flew four top chefs over specially from Sichuan, and our restaurant has gone from strength to strength.' No wonder, and well done David! So you can see that it really pays to have a sense of what you want to do. On the other hand, Sarah Robson at Ely gets her inspiration from much closer to home. 'We try to keep the food simple, Irish and traditional wherever possible . . . the dishes I've chosen reflect the rich, no-frills style of food that we do here at Ely.' You mean, like the 'honey roast organic shank of lamb on a bed of creamed potatoes with caramelised shallots and red currants'? Yeah, I sure like the sound of that one Sarah, keep it up!

The Dublin restaurant scene also owes a lot to the French. I don't just mean the two Frenchmen that our fair city has managed to capture the hearts of – Jacques Carrera and Sebastien Masi. We're so lucky to have charmed them away from a country where, as

Jacques says, they were 'born into food' and where 'eating is a lifestyle – like stout for the Irish'. We appreciate their knowledge and skills and the way they have shared them so generously in Dublin. What I also mean is that many of our chefs have had the good fortune to have superb French training and technique. Many of them have trained in some of the very best French kitchens in the world. The French technique is often quite obvious, even though many describe their cooking as modern Irish. How come? It's quite simple really. Many of the French techniques and skills are so sound and sensible that they have been absorbed by nearly every Western restaurant culture. Then you add to this solid basis the beautiful Irish ingredients, a bit of Celtic spirit and the artistic Irish sense, and there you have it. Even Sebastien Masi has been seduced: 'blue lobster with sautéed potatoes flambéed in Irish whiskey'. That's modern Irish cooking to me. Similarly, Ross Lewis cooks my favourite fish in the whole world, Irish turbot. It's a dish with heavy French influence, but with the accompaniment of champ, broad beans and smoked bacon it's definitely Irish too. I like what Ross says in his profile: 'Ireland, true to its reputation, encourages the artistic spirit.'

Finally, I just want to mention one important aspect of the restaurant business that is often forgotten, and that is hospitality. A perfect meal served without a smile or a generous spirit is not worth having. I've always thought that a great chef must have a generous nature. To work tirelessly day in and day out, giving their all to every single plate, is almost the work of a saint, but that is what they do. It should be balanced by someone equally dedicated and generous in the dining room, and even on the telephone. Luckily, in Ireland we tend to have hospitality in our blood, and it is mostly smiles and sincere charm that is found in our restaurants. However, it's actually one of our imported Frenchmen who has said it best: 'We make a point of avoiding the fuss and flurry that so many other restaurants are prone to now, and go out of our way to ensure that every single customer feels cherished and as comfortable as if dining in their own home.' That is the type of hospitality you get from Jacques Carrera at La Mère Zou. I can't wait to go back!

Bon appetit everyone!

Post Office, O'Connell Street

New Recipes from
Dublin's Finest Chefs

Avoca Café

JOHN DUNNE

I began cooking at the age of fifteen and throughout my twenty-three-year career working mainly in Michelin-rated restaurants I have been lucky enough to work for some brilliant and talented chefs – the likes of Sonia Stephenson, Raymond Blanc and John Burton-Race. Of all of them, I think it was probably John who instilled in me the greatest understanding of food and cooking.

I started working at Avoca Café in September 2001 and love the buzz – both inside the kitchen and out. It's very much about people enjoying themselves, ideal for families and with the emphasis on excellent food and service. So whether it's a plate of refreshing salad, a grilled dish or a tasty dessert, we aim to make it special.

My philosophy has always been to rely on the freshest and highest quality seasonal ingredients, treated simply to show them off to their best advantage. This is reflected in the food I serve at Avoca Café, where our style is modern European with contemporary global influences.

I have chosen the following recipes as they are my current favourites, summing up my style of cooking whilst working brilliantly together as a simple and refreshing menu. The wild mushroom tart is one of the best hot starters you'll ever try, the sweet leeks, the nutty flavour of the mushrooms, the crispy pastry and the balsamic onions all combining to make a simple yet mouth-watering dish. The crispiness of the salad that follows complements the meatiness of the tuna, with the sesame, coriander and noodles finishing the dish perfectly, and what can I say about the raspberry and lemon dessert? Heavenly.

AVOCA CAFÉ

Starter

Wild mushroom tart
with leeks and balsamic onions

Wine suggestion: Gewürztraminer Reserve,
2000, Gustave Lorentz, Alsace (France)

Main course

Tuna loin fillets
with a sesame-dressed salad and
wilted pak choi

Wine suggestion: Lawson's Dry Hill Sauvignon
Blanc, 2000 (New Zealand)

Dessert

Burnt lemon cream
with raspberries

Wine suggestion: Château Court-les-Mûts,
1999, Bergerac (France)

Menu

Wild mushroom tart

with leeks and balsamic onions

for the savoury pastry
cases
225g plain flour
150g unsalted butter,
diced
$1/2$ tsp salt
1–2 egg yolks

for the filling
400g mixed wild
mushrooms

8 tbsp extra virgin olive
oil
1 large pinch of fresh
thyme, finely chopped
1 large pinch of fresh
tarragon, finely
chopped
2 cloves of garlic, finely
chopped
salt and freshly ground
black pepper

3 small leeks, well
washed and sliced
12 onions in balsamic
(available from a
delicatessen)

for the garnish
110g Parmesan Reggiano
cheese, thinly shaved
chives

For the savoury pastry cases: Sift the flour into a bowl and, using your fingertips, rub in the butter until the mixture resembles fine breadcrumbs. Stir in the salt and then mix in enough of the egg yolks to give a soft dough, adding a little cold water if you run out of egg yolk. Wrap the pastry in cling film and leave it to rest in the fridge for 20–30 minutes.

Preheat the oven to 180°C (gas mark 4). Roll the pastry out thinly on a lightly floured work surface and use it to line 4 tart tins, 10cm in diameter. Bake the cases in the oven for 15–20 minutes until they are golden brown, then allow them to cool before removing them from the tins.

For the filling: Carefully clean the mushrooms, cutting the larger ones in half, and gently fry them in a pan with the oil, herbs and garlic until they are tender. Season the mushrooms with salt and pepper, remove them from the pan and set them aside to keep warm. Return the pan the mushrooms were cooked in to the heat and add the leeks. Cook them over a moderate heat until they are tender and then season them. Meanwhile, warm the pastry cases and the onions through in a warm oven then fill the tarts with the mushroom mixture.

To serve, arrange some of the warm leeks in the centre of each of the 4 serving plates. Place the mushroom-filled tarts on top, with the Parmesan shavings scattered over them and some chives across the top. Arrange the warmed onions around the edge and present them immediately.

Tuna loin fillets
with a sesame-dressed salad and wilted pok choi

for the sesame dressing
300ml sesame oil
75ml rice wine vinegar
25g sesame seeds, toasted
juice and finely grated zest of 1 lime
salt and freshly ground black pepper

for the salad
1 x 200g punnet of bean sprouts
2 medium red peppers, finely sliced
2 medium carrots, peeled and very
    finely sliced
200g rice noodles

5 spring onions, finely chopped
1 small bunch of fresh coriander, finely
    chopped

for the tuna loin fillets
4 x 200g tuna loin fillets
salt and freshly ground black pepper
a little extra virgin olive oil

for the garnish
1 bunch of baby pok choi
2 lemons, cut in half

For the sesame dressing: Whisk all the ingredients together and check the seasoning. Pour the dressing into a screw-top jar and, before serving, shake it well.

For the salad: Cook the noodles for 1 minute in boiling water and allow them to drain. Then mix all the ingredients together in a large bowl.

For the tuna loin fillets: Preheat a griddle pan, sauté pan or barbecue to a high heat. Season the tuna loin fillets with the salt and black pepper and smear each one with a little olive oil to prevent them sticking. Cook the fish to your liking. If you prefer your tuna rare, I suggest you cook it for approximately 2–3 minutes on each side, depending on the thickness of the fillets. Increase the cooking time on each side by a minute or so for a more well-done finish.

For the garnish: Wilt the pok choi by lightly grilling it on both sides for about 25 seconds. You could also place the lemon halves cut side down on a heated griddle for a char-grilled effect.

To serve, dress the salad with the sesame dressing, divide it between the 4 serving plates and place a tuna loin fillet on top. Garnish each plate with a little wilted pok choi and half a lemon and present the dish immediately.

Burnt lemon cream
with raspberries

juice of 4 lemons
165g caster sugar
zest of 2 lemons, finely grated
6 eggs
350ml double cream
28 raspberries

for the garnish
a little icing sugar, for dusting
shortbread biscuits

Preheat the oven to 180°C (gas mark 4). Boil up the lemon juice with the sugar to make a syrup and allow this to cool. Put the eggs into a bowl, pour the lemon syrup over them and whisk the eggs and syrup together. Bring the cream to the boil and then whisk it into the egg and lemon mixture, together with the lemon zest. Pour the mixture into 4 white ovenproof dishes, about 11cm in diameter, and plop 6 raspberries into each. Place the dishes on an oven tray, put it in the oven and cook the creams for about 20 minutes or until they are set. Remove the dishes from the oven, leave them to cool and then put them in the fridge until they are chilled.

To serve, dust each of the lemon creams with icing sugar, caramelise them either under a hot grill or with a blowtorch and garnish each with a raspberry and some shortbread biscuits.

Bachelor's Walk

Cavistons Seafood Restaurant

PETER CAVISTON

Running Cavistons is a far cry from delivering fish by bike as a messenger boy in my youth. But then again, I guess that one thing does remain the same – the seafood. My family has run Cavistons Food Emporium for over fifty years, so there's not much we don't know about seafood. But it was still a big step for us to open a restaurant because we had such an excellent reputation to maintain. But open one we did, and the rest, as they say, is history.

The most important thing for us is freshness. Our menu is based around the day's catch so that it tastes as if it's just been brought in by the Irish fishing fleet. What comes in on the day, we sell on the day – nothing fancy, nothing complicated, just simple, fresh food that speaks for itself.

Like the tian of crab which follows, a light and refreshing way to start any meal with its avocado and red onion salsa cutting through the richness of the local crab – perfect with a cool glass of elegant Sauvignon Blanc. It also prepares the palate for the main course, the seafood selection complete with chargrilled Dublin Bay prawns. And with the millefeuille of Irish strawberries to end the meal, you'll be perfectly set up for whatever the rest of the evening has to offer.

So eat fish and live longer. (And if you manage to have a couple of glasses of wine a day too, so much the better!)

CAVISTONS SEAFOOD RESTAURANT

Starter

Tian of West of Ireland crab
with an avocado and red onion salsa

Wine suggestion: Sancerre, Sauvignon Blanc,
1998, Domaine André Dézat (France)

Main course

Chargrilled Dublin Bay prawns
with langoustines and crab claws

Wine suggestion: Pouilly-Fumé, 1998/9,
Domaine André Dézat (France)

Dessert

Millefeuille of Irish strawberries
with summer fruit coulis and crème
pâtissière

Wine suggestion: Sauternes, 2ème Cru, 1995,
Château Filhot (France)

Menu

Tian of West of Ireland crab

with an avocado and red onion salsa

for the crab
225g white crab meat
2 tbsp mayonnaise (readymade is fine)
juice of 2 lemons
freshly ground black pepper

for the avocado and red onion salsa
2 avocados, diced
1 red onion, peeled and diced

1 chilli, chopped
$^{1}/_{2}$ tsp fresh coriander, chopped
a little virgin olive oil

for the garnish
2 cherry tomatoes, halved
a little balsamic vinegar
flat-leaf parsley and chives

For the crab: Mix all the ingredients together.

For the avocado and red onion salsa: Mix all the ingredients together.

To serve, place a tian, pastry cutter or something similar in the centre of a serving plate. Put a quarter of the crab meat mixture into it and top this off with a quarter of the avocado and red onion salsa. Remove the tian and repeat the process for the other 3 plates. Place a cherry tomato half on each plate, drizzle a little balsamic vinegar over and garnish with the fresh herbs.

Chargrilled Dublin Bay prawns
with langoustines and crab claws

for the Dublin Bay prawns
600–700g fresh Dublin Bay prawns
2 tbsp virgin olive oil
a pinch of rock salt
2 tsp fresh parsley, chopped

for the langoustines and crab claws
$1/2$ tsp blackened Cajun seasoning
   (readymade is fine)
25g unsalted butter, brought to room
   temperature

4 ready-cooked langoustines
8 ready-cooked crab claws

for the garnish
1 lemon, cut into wedges
4 sprigs of fresh parsley or dill

for the accompaniments
boiled baby French potatoes
mixed green salad leaves

For the Dublin Bay prawns: Heat the grill to a high temperature, put the prawns under it and cook them for 5–10 minutes, turning them occasionally as they cook. Place the prawns on a hot flat baking tray. Add the olive oil, rock salt and parsley and put the prawns back under the grill for a further 2–3 minutes.

For the langoustines and crab claws: Mix the Cajun seasoning into the butter and melt the mixture in a heavy-based frying pan over a low heat. Cook the langoustines and crab claws in the seasoned butter for a few minutes, until they are warmed through.

   To serve, either arrange the seafood on a platter as shown, or divide it up between the serving plates with the garnishes and accompaniments as required.

Millefeuille of Irish strawberries
with summer fruit coulis and crème pâtissière

for the pastry
225g puff pastry (readymade is fine)

for the crème pâtissière
570ml full cream milk
1 vanilla pod, split
4 egg yolks
75g caster sugar
40g plain flour

for the summer fruit coulis
about 225g mixed fresh summer fruits
caster sugar to taste

for the garnish
1 punnet of strawberries, hulled and
  sliced

For the pastry: Preheat the oven to 200°C (gas mark 6). Roll out the pastry to a thickness of about 2cm and cut it into discs using an 8cm pastry cutter. Put the discs on a greased baking sheet and bake them in the oven for 8–10 minutes. Remove the pastry discs from the oven and allow them to cool.

For the crème pâtissière: Put the milk and the split vanilla pod into a pan, bring them to the boil and then remove the pan from the heat. Beat the egg yolks and sugar together in a mixing bowl. Pour the hot milk over, add the flour and mix well. Pour this mixture back into the pan, put it over a moderate heat and cook until the mixture thickens. Remove the pan from the heat and leave the mixture to cool.

For the summer fruits coulis: Put the fruit and sugar into a pan and simmer over a moderate heat for a few minutes, until the fruit is soft. Remove the pan from the heat and strain the coulis to remove the skin, pips and seeds and make a smooth fruit sauce.

To serve, cut the pastry discs in half, spread the bottom half of each with the crème pâtissière and arrange some strawberry slices on top. Place the pastry tops on like lids and drizzle the summer fruit coulis around the edge along with any remaining crème pâtissière.

St Stephen's Green

Chapter One

ROSS LEWIS

I started working at Chapter One in 1992, having trained in a succession of restaurants all over the world. Unlike many chefs, my family background didn't draw me into the trade, but I had a natural affiliation to food, combined with a disposition well suited to the demands of a people-orientated business. I love the land and have a great respect for all aspects of the food industry, especially artisans who put their hearts and souls into creating quality produce. Ireland, true to its reputation, encourages the artistic spirit. The people are generous in their praise when they feel someone is making a genuine effort, and coming back home to Ireland has given me an opportunity to establish myself professionally.

The dishes I've selected for this book represent summer food at its best, not to mention including some classic Irish ingredients like Atlantic lobster and champ, typical of Chapter One's menu. Here, fine produce, cooked simply and with care, come together to create hearty dishes which respect the main ingredients. The sweet, sweet lobster flesh in the starter sings above the citrus fruit consommé, while virgin olive oil adds depth and richness. Try sipping a glass of Baron de Ladoucette Chablis 1998 and see how its buttery, nutty flavours complement the lobster while its freshness and acidity match the flavours of the broth. Then comes the succulent roasted turbot, with its earthy champ, robust red wine fumet and smoky, salty bacon, reflected perfectly in the Chambolle Musigny, 1999. And to bring the meal to a sumptuous close, the dessert combines the richness of melting chocolate with crème brûlée and a light basil ice cream – ingredients that sing out loud but in harmony, especially when tasted with the balancing fifteen-year-old Mas Amiel Maury.

I recommend them all to you as epitomising the best of Chapter One's modern Irish food, not to mention the originality and authenticity of the people who have helped to bring them about. Enjoy!

CHAPTER ONE

Starter

Warm lobster served in a citrus and
vegetable consommé
with virgin olive oil and asparagus tips

Wine suggestion: Chablis, 1998, Baron Patrick,
Baron de Ladoucette (France)

Main course

Roast turbot
with champ, red wine fumet, celeriac,
caramelised shallots, broad beans and
smoked bacon

Wine suggestion: Chambolle Musigny, 1999,
Domaine A. Hudelot-Noellat (France)

Dessert

Warm chocolate fondant
with crème brûlée ravioli, basil ice cream
and orange sauce

Wine suggestion: Mas Amiel Maury
(15-year-old)

Menu

Warm lobster
served in a citrus and vegetable consommé
with virgin olive oil and asparagus tips

The lobster is the queen of the sea. In this dish, her sweetness and flavour shine
out from a backdrop of citrus and olive oil. This dish offers sweetness, acidity and
richness – light and perfect! The vegetable nage should be made the day before
serving.

for the vegetable nage
1 head of fennel, chopped
2 carrots, chopped
1 leek, chopped
3 sticks of celery, chopped
1 bay leaf
5 peppercorns, crushed
2 litre still mineral water

for the lobster
2 x 500g fresh Atlantic lobsters

for the asparagus
20 asparagus tips

for the citrus and vegetable
   consommé
600ml vegetable nage, made the day
   before
1 lime, segmented
1 orange, segmented
$1/2$ lemon, segmented
$1/2$ pink grapefruit, segmented
50ml cold-pressed virgin olive oil
   (Spanish D. O. Baena or similar
   quality)
sea salt and freshly ground white
   pepper

for the garnish
20g fresh chervil

For the vegetable nage: Bring all the ingredients to the boil, then turn down the
heat and simmer for 40 minutes. Allow the nage to cool, cover it and leave it in the
fridge overnight. Strain the nage, bring it back to the boil and reduce it to 600ml.

For the lobsters: Bring a pan of salted water to the boil and, when it reaches a
simmering temperature of 70°C (130°F), put the lobsters into the water and cook
them at this temperature for 8 minutes. Take the lobsters out of the pan and
extract the meat, which should be slightly undercooked, from the claws and tails.
Divide each tail into 4 to give 8 separate tail pieces and 4 claw pieces.

For the asparagus: Blanch the asparagus tips for $2^1/2$ minutes in salted water and
then refresh them in iced water.

For the citrus and vegetable consommé: Once the nage is reduced to about 600ml, add the citrus fruit segments and boil them for 2 minutes. Add the portioned lobster and simmer for a further minute. Add the olive oil and, after another 30 seconds, the asparagus tips. Season and remove the pan from the heat.

To serve, put 5 asparagus tips, 1 lobster claw and 2 pieces of lobster tail into each of 4 shallow bowls. Then pour over the citrus and vegetable consommé and garnish with chervil.

Roast turbot

with champ, red wine fumet, celeriac, caramelised shallots, broad beans and smoked bacon

This really is a hearty dish – the red wine, smoked bacon and creamy potato spiked with spring onion are all big on taste but the turbot is strong enough to triumph. Absolutely delicious! You'll have to start the day before serving, though, as the shallots need to be marinated overnight.

for the caramelised shallots
40g brown sugar
400ml red wine
1 bay leaf
2 star anise
12 small shallots, peeled and whole
40g unsalted butter
salt and freshly ground black pepper

for the red wine fumet
4 shallots, chopped
50g mushrooms, sliced
10ml light olive oil
300ml red wine (cabernet sauvignon if possible)
200ml fish or mussel stock (readymade is fine)
200ml chicken stock (readymade is fine) – alternatively, use

400ml chicken stock in place of the fish stock and chicken stock
1 sprig of fresh thyme
1 sprig of fresh rosemary
1 sprig of fresh parsley
1 sprig of fresh tarragon
1 bay leaf
5 black peppercorns
100ml double cream
1 tbsp unsalted butter
salt and freshly ground white pepper

For the caramelised shallots: Mix the sugar into the red wine in a bowl and add the bay leaf, star anise and the shallots. Cover the bowl and leave the shallots to marinate overnight in the fridge.

Preheat the oven to 170°C (gas mark 3). Remove the shallots from the marinade and put them in a casserole with the butter, salt and pepper. Put the lid on the casserole and bake in the oven for about 10–15 minutes until the shallots are semi-soft. Remove the lid and bake for a further 10 minutes, turning the shallots occasionally so that they are glazed.

For the red wine fumet: Place the shallots and mushrooms in a pan with the olive oil and fry them until the onions are transparent. Add all the other ingredients, except the cream, butter, salt and white pepper, and simmer until the liquid is reduced by about two-thirds. Add the cream and reduce by a third. Strain through a fine chinois or preferably muslin cloth. Reboil the fumet with the butter and finish with the salt and pepper.

for the champ

4 medium-sized rooster
  potatoes
400ml double cream,
  reduced to 200ml
80g unsalted butter,
  cubed and chilled
6 spring onions, finely
  chopped
sea salt and freshly
  ground white pepper

for the celeriac

200ml milk
200ml water
1 celeriac, cut into 2cm
  dice
salt and freshly ground
  white pepper
a squeeze of lemon juice

for the turbot

4 x 160g fresh turbot
  fillets
sea salt and freshly
  ground white pepper

a little light olive oil
1 tbsp unsalted butter
a squeeze of lemon juice

for the accompaniments

20 broad beans,
  blanched and shelled
1 tbsp olive oil
1 tbsp water
sea salt and freshly
  ground white pepper
4 thin slices of smoked
  bacon, grilled and
  crispy

For the champ: Boil the potatoes in salted water in their skins. Allow them to cool, peel them and push the cooked potato through a fine sieve. In a small pan, warm the cream and spring onions to bring the flavour of the spring onions through. Add the sieved potato and work it into the cream with a plastic spatula. Gradually add the chilled butter, working it in until you have a smooth purée. Season the champ with the sea salt and white pepper and put it aside to keep warm.

For the celeriac: Mix the milk and water together in a saucepan, add 16 pieces of the diced celeriac and bring it to the boil. Simmer for 3–4 minutes, until the celeriac is tender. Drain the celeriac, season with the salt and pepper and add the lemon juice.

For the turbot: Season the turbot fillets with salt and pepper and sauté over a medium heat in the olive oil and butter for approximately 3 minutes on each side. Finish with a squeeze of lemon juice.

To serve, put the olive oil and water into a pan with the salt and pepper and re-warm the broad beans and celeriac over a medium heat for 2–3 minutes. Divide the champ into 4 equal portions and place a portion in the middle of each of the 4 serving plates. Put a turbot fillet on top and arrange 3 glazed shallots, 4 cubes of celeriac and 5 broad beans around each plate. Pour some of the red wine fumet over the fish, drizzle some more around the champ and finish the dish by placing a crispy smoked bacon piece on the top.

Warm chocolate fondant

with crème brûlée ravioli, basil ice cream and orange sauce

In this recipe you will need to make the crème brûlée the night before to allow it to chill.

for the crème brûlée
  ravioli
5 egg yolks
70g caster sugar
100ml full cream milk
300ml double cream
1 vanilla pod, split
8 wonton skins
a little icing sugar

for the basil ice cream
40 fresh basil leaves

zest of 1 orange
180g caster sugar
12 egg yolks
600ml full cream milk
400ml double cream

for the chocolate
  fondant
3 whole eggs
150g caster sugar
80g callibaut chocolate
  (any good dark 70%

cocoa solids chocolate
  is fine), melted
100g unsalted butter,
  melted and cooled
40g plain flour

for the orange sauce
juice of 4 oranges
100ml Grand Marnier
1 vanilla pod, split and
  deseeded
30g caster sugar

For the crème brûlée: Preheat the oven to 100°C. Put the egg yolks and sugar into a bowl and whisk them together vigorously. Put the milk, cream and vanilla pod into a thick-bottomed pan, bring it to the boil and simmer for 3 minutes. Add about one-third of this to the egg and sugar mixture and beat well. Now pour this all back into the pan with the rest of the hot milk and cream and mix everything together. Take the pan off the heat, remove the vanilla pod, and pour the mixture into 4 ramekins or small ovenproof dishes. Bake them in the oven for 40 minutes. Please note that it is important not to have the oven temperature higher than 100°C as this will result in the eggs becoming scrambled. Remove the ramekins from the oven and allow them to cool, before putting them in the fridge overnight to chill.

For the basil ice cream: Using a pestle and mortar, grind up the basil and orange zest with half of the sugar. Whisk the remaining sugar into the egg yolks and beat well. Boil together the milk and cream, add about one-third of this to the egg and sugar mixture and mix well. Pour the mixture into the pan with the remaining hot milk and cream, add the basil, orange zest and sugar mixture and again mix well. Return the pan to the heat and, stirring continuously, cook the mixture until it

thickens and coats the back of a spoon. Allow the mixture to cool and then churn it in an ice cream maker.

For the chocolate fondant: Preheat the oven to 180°C (gas mark 4). Beat the eggs and sugar together to form a sabayon. Add the melted chocolate, the butter and the sieved flour and mix everything together. Take 4 chilled dariole moulds and grease them well with softened butter, ensuring all surfaces are well coated. Now lightly dust the moulds with flour to prevent the cooked fondants from sticking, pour the mixture in and bake the fondants for 8 minutes in the oven.

For the ravioli: Drop the wonton skins into boiling water and cook them for $1^1/_2$ minutes. Remove them from the water, place each one on the work surface and put 1 teaspoon of the chilled brûlée mixture on to 4 of them. Cover each with another skin and seal them by pressing the edges together with your fingers to form 4 ravioli parcels. Sprinkle them with icing sugar and put them under a hot grill for half a minute.

For the orange sauce: Place all ingredients in a pan over a moderate heat and allow the volume to reduce by about one-third.

To serve, upturn the dariole moulds over the centre of 4 serving plates and allow the chocolate fondants to slide out. Place a crème brûlée ravioli next to each, together with a generous scoop of basil ice cream, and drizzle the orange sauce around them.

Trinity College

China Sichuan Restaurant

DAVID HUI

China Sichuan Restaurant is a family business so I guess that cooking has always been in my blood. We opened our doors for the first time in 1986 – a bold step to take, as at the time oriental cuisine in both Ireland and the UK was dominated by Cantonese-based food, the unique combinations of flavour and texture in Sichuan cooking remaining undiscovered. But we took the bull by the horns, flew four top chefs over specially from Sichuan, and our restaurant has gone from strength to strength.

Part of our success lies in the consistency of our food. And to ensure that each dish we serve is of the highest standard possible, we import the likes of the Sichuan vinegar, peppercorns and garlic sauce direct from Sichuan as the flavours are more rich and pungent than their European counterparts.

We have chosen what are probably the most popular dishes on our menu for you here. Bang Bang Ji (chicken) originates from a small village outside Chengdu, its name deriving from the way the locals beat the chicken meat loose with wooden sticks so that it can be torn apart easily and then tossed in a variety of different dressings. Try this with a light, aromatic wine like a Muscat Sec from the Côtes Catalanes – a floral wine that is just so easy to drink! Follow this with our award-winning signature dish, Yu Xiang Rou Si, or Fried Pork Shreds in Garlic Sauce, and a glass or two of a good crisp white like Collavini's Pinot Grigio to bring out the rich ginger and garlic flavours. (Alternatively, a Gewürztraminer always complements this type of food well, although finding a good bottle with the right balance of flavours and lovely fresh lychee tones can be tricky – especially at the right price.) And to round off the perfect Sichuan experience, try creating our Glazed Caramel Bananas and reward yourself with a glass of Tokaji as you bite into the hot crisp caramel.

Our chefs: Guilian Zou (far left – just out of shot), Jiang Li, Qicona Chen, Jian Liao and Head Chef Qizhi Chen (right)

CHINA SICHUAN RESTAURANT

Starter

Bang Bang Ji (Chicken)

Wine suggestion: Muscat Sec, 2000, Vin de Pays
des Côtes Catalanes, Domaine Piquemal
(France)

Main course

Yu Xiang Rou Si
(Fried pork shreds in a garlic sauce)

Wine suggestion: Pinot Grigio, Collavini, Friuli
(Italian)

Dessert

Glazed caramel bananas

Wine suggestion: Royal Tokaji Aszu Five
Puttonyos, 1996, Royal Tokaji Wine Company
(Hungary)

Menu

Bang-bang ji
(Bang-bang chicken)

This is a fairly quick and simple starter to make and is meant to be served cold.

for the chicken
3 x 200g fresh skinless chicken breasts

for the sauce
4 tbsp light Soya sauce
2 tbsp Sichuan vinegar (Chinese black
    vinegar is fine)
15g granulated sugar
15g sesame paste

5g sesame seeds, roasted and crushed
1 tsp chilli oil
$1/2$ tsp ground roasted Sichuan
    peppercorns
1 tsp sesame oil

for the accompaniments
20g iceberg lettuce, chopped
5g scallions, chopped

For the chicken: Boil the chicken breasts for 30–35 minutes until they are cooked through. Tear or cut the chicken into shreds approximately 3–4cm in length. (The real method would be to hit the chicken a few times with a wooden stick until the meat starts loosening up and then to tear it into little strips, using your hands.)

For the sauce: Thoroughly mix all the ingredients together.

To serve, place a small mound of lettuce in the centre of each of the 4 serving plates. Arrange some chicken shreds on top and pour the sauce over it. Finally, scatter the scallions over the dish.

Yu Xiang Rou Si

(Fried pork shreds in a garlic sauce)

Also called fish-flavoured pork shreds, this dish has to be one of our favourites and it is probably one of the most famous dishes from Sichuan. Fish-flavoured dishes are dishes in which the ingredients and spices used are more usually associated with the preparation of seafood. We make our own Sichuan garlic sauce and import our own vinegar from Sichuan, but similar versions are available in your nearest Chinese supermarket.

for the marinade	for the sauce	2 tbsp Sichuan vinegar
1 egg white	10g fresh ginger, finely	1 tbsp light soya sauce
15g cornflour	chopped	5g cornflour mixed with
a pinch of salt	10g garlic, finely	4 tbsp water
1 tbsp water	chopped	50g scallions, chopped
	15g Sichuan garlic sauce	
for the pork	1 tsp Shaoxing wine	for the
200g pork steaks or	(any white cooking	accompaniments
tenderloin of pork	wine is fine)	steamed rice
75ml vegetable oil	15g granulated sugar	parsley, to garnish

For the marinade: Thoroughly mix all the ingredients together.

For the pork: Slice the pork very thinly and then cut the slices into very narrow strips. Put the pork strips into a bowl with the marinade, mix thoroughly and leave for 5 minutes. Put a wok on a high heat and pour in the vegetable oil. When the oil is hot enough (that is, when it starts to smoke), add the pork and stir-fry quickly until the pork turns white in colour – expect this to take around 30–45 seconds. Drain off the excess oil by tipping the wok to the side.

For the sauce: Place the ginger, garlic and garlic sauce in the wok, stirring until the oil turns red and you can smell the garlic and ginger. Add the wine, then a mixture of the sugar, vinegar, soya sauce and cornflour in water and stir-fry for a further minute. Finally add the scallions, stir-fry for another 10 seconds and serve immediately with steamed rice and a parsley garnish.

Glazed caramel bananas

These deep-fried bananas coated in hot caramel look simple and they are. The only trick is to make sure that everything you need for the final stage is ready because you do need to work very quickly just prior to serving.

for the batter
200g self-raising flour
1 egg, beaten
1 tsp vegetable oil
about 200ml water

for the bananas
2 bananas

for the caramel
150ml water
150g granulated sugar
1 tbsp vegetable oil

for the accompaniment
vanilla ice cream

For the batter: Combine all the ingredients, adding just enough water to give the consistency of thick cream.

For the bananas: Preheat the oil in the deep-fat fryer to 200°C. Peel the bananas and cut each of them into 8 equal pieces. Dip the pieces of banana into the batter mixture and deep fry until they are crisp and golden. Remove them from the oil, drain them on some kitchen paper and leave them aside for the moment. Keep the oil hot as you will need to reheat the bananas in it.

For the caramel: Mix the sugar with the water and heat the mixture in a wok or frying pan over a moderate heat, stirring constantly until the sugar dissolves and the mixture turns golden in colour. The caramel should now be of a nice flowing treacly consistency. When the water is nearly reduced, add the oil and mix well. Remove the caramel from the heat and continue stirring. Keep the caramel hot in the wok.

To serve, have a bowl of iced water and a greased serving dish at the ready. Reheat the bananas by quickly deep-frying them again for a minute or so. Remove the bananas from the fryer and immediately dip them into the hot caramel, gently moving them around until they are completely coated. Quickly plunge the caramel-coated bananas into the bowl of iced water to harden the caramel, take them out again quickly using a slotted spoon and place them on the greased serving dish with a scoop of ice cream.

G.C.S.
086
2745045

BEAD

Bachelor's Walk

& CRYSTALS

By
Yellow
Brick
Road

YELLOW
BRICK
ROAD

OPENING HOURS
10.30 - 6.00
MON. - SAT.

Dunne & Crescenzi

EILEEN DUNNE CRESCENZI

I became involved in cooking as a natural extension of my love affair with Italy. Whilst studying at the Accademia delle Belli Arti in Rome, I loved to go to the typical trattorie (family-run restaurants) around the Trastevere and San Lorenzo areas of the city and fell in love with the simplicity of the cuisine – a passion I share with my Italian husband Stefano. We met while I was working with the United Nations and we travelled all over the country together, seeking out the regional specialities and traditions behind the food.

Perhaps the biggest influence on my formation as a chef, however, was Stefano's grandmother, Nonna Valentina. She was a formidable cook and excessively proud of her Roman roots, and she talked incessantly about the city's cuisine, divulging little secrets here and there that made each dish that little bit more special.

Inspired by this, I started Dunne & Crescenzi in December 1999 – just in time for the Christmas rush. Keeping things simple and informal, we offer fine Italian food in a friendly and relaxed atmosphere – as if our customers are guests in our own home. After all, food and wine do bring people together, and I've been told that people leave the place feeling that they've just been to Italy!

I chose the dishes that follow because they are typical representations of Roman cuisine. The pasta is a substantial and satisfying starter which, like both main courses, works well with a Frascati Superiore like Ponticello from Pallavicini – although personally I prefer a nice Tuscan red like Morellino di Scansano from Castelli del Grevepesa. The pasta should be followed by a light tasty dish like Saltimbocca together with the artichokes, which clean the palate and aid digestion, while the Torta di Ricotta is a wonderful finish to any meal – any left-overs making a tasty addition to afternoon tea or, in true Italian style, breakfast! Perhaps avoid the Moscato from Cantina d' Isera first thing in the morning, though!

So pour yourself a glass of good Prosecco, bring out the olives and relax into a virtual Italian experience.

DUNNE & CRESCENZI

Starter

Bucatini all'Amatriciana

Wine suggestion: Ponticello, Frascati Superiore,
Pallavicini, Lazio (Italy)

Main course

Saltimbocca
with carciofi alla Romana

Wine suggestion: Morellino di Scansano,
Castelli del Grevepesa, Tuscany (Italy)

Dessert

Crostata di ricotta

Wine suggestion: Moscato, Cantina d'Isera,
Trentino (Italy)

Menu

Bucatini all'Amatriciana

A great favourite with all Romans, Bucatini all'Amatriciana is a pasta dish that comes from the town of Amatrice in Lazio.

for the sauce	for the pasta
4 tbsp Italian extra virgin olive oil	400g Bucatini pasta
1 small onion, finely chopped	2 litres boiling water
110g guanciale (cured pork cheeks) or	20g salt
pancetta, diced	50g pecorino cheese, finely grated
2 tbsp balsamic vinegar or wine	50g Parmesan cheese, finely grated
vinegar	
700ml organic passata or 2 tins	
(average size) cherry tomatoes	
salt, to taste	

For the sauce: Place the olive oil, guanciale (or pancetta) and onion in a saucepan and fry gently for a few minutes until the onion softens but does not change colour. Add the balsamic vinegar and turn the heat up for 10 seconds. Lower the heat again, add the tomatoes and salt and cook the sauce uncovered for 20 minutes on a moderate heat, stirring occassionally.

For the pasta: Pasta should always be cooked in plenty of boiling water so use a large, tall saucepan for cooking it. The rule is at least half a litre of water for every 100g of pasta so, in this case, we require at least 2 litres of water. I say at least because it is wiser to err on the side of too much water rather than too little. (Too little water will make the pasta gooey.) I usually put the salt in the water – 10g for every litre – before I put the saucepan on the cooker, just in case I forget later on.

Add the pasta to the boiling salted water and stir gently to ensure that all of the pasta is covered by water. Continue to stir every few minutes to prevent it sticking together. The pasta is cooked according to the cooking time indicated on the packet but remember that one minute less is always better than one minute more! Drain the pasta and put it into a serving bowl. Add the two grated cheeses and stir so that all the pasta becomes coated in cheese. Add the sauce, mix gently and serve immediately. Buon appetito!

Saltimbocca
with carciofi alla Romana

Saltimbocca means 'jump in the mouth' and that's very appropriate for this dish because it's so tasty. Carciofi conjures up wonderful images of stalls in the Roman markets, weighed down under mountains of green and purple artichokes.

for the carciofi alla Romana
2 cloves of garlic, crushed
1 handful of fresh parsley, chopped
1 handful of fresh mint, chopped
4 large artichokes (romaneschi)
4 tbsp Italian extra virgin olive oil
$^1/_2$ a glass of dry white wine.
salt, to taste
about $^1/_2$ a cup of hot water

for the saltimbocca
8 thin slices of Parma ham
8 fresh sage leaves
4 x 100g veal steaks, very thin and
   tender
8 tbsp Italian extra virgin olive oil
8 tbsp dry white wine
salt and freshly ground black pepper

For the carciofi alla Romana: Mix the garlic, parsley and mint together. Remove all the tough outer leaves from the artichokes and scoop out the furry beards from the centre. Chop across at least 2.5cm from the tops to remove the jagged edges, then cut and scrape the stalks to about 3cm. Hold the artichokes in one hand by the stalk and, with the other hand, open the leaves at the top and stuff the centres with the garlic, parsley and mint mixture. Heat the olive oil in a saucepan and put the artichokes in, heads down and with the stalks standing up. Fry them gently for about 3 minutes, then add the wine and then the salt and hot water. Cover the pan and simmer for around 20–30 minutes or until the artichokes are tender. Check the pan from time to time and, if it looks too dry, add a little extra water.

For the saltimbocca: Place a slice of Parma ham and a fresh sage leaf on each veal steak and secure with a toothpick. Cook the veal steaks in two batches heating half of the olive oil in a wide pan and adding the prepared veal steaks. Fry them lightly on a moderate heat for 2 minutes and then turn them over and fry them for a further 2 minutes. Add 4 tablespoons of the wine and cook the meat for another minute, turning it over occasionally. Repeat with the second batch of steaks. Add salt and pepper to taste.

To serve, place the veal steaks on a warmed serving dish, add the juices from the pan and present the dish with the carciofi.

Crostata di ricotta

There is a wonderful small bakery in the Jewish Quarter of Rome behind the synagogue where they make the best crostata di ricotta.

for the ricotta filling
600g ricotta cheese
300g granulated sugar
4 free range eggs
grated rind of 1 lemon
grated rind of 1 orange
50g good quality dark
  chocolate
50g pinoli pine nuts
50g candied fruit
  (optional)

a pinch of ground
  cinnamon
1 eggcup measure of
  brandy

for the pastry
300g plain flour
3 free range eggs
150g unsalted butter,
  cut into cubes
300g granulated sugar

a pinch of salt
grated rind of 1 lemon
1 free range egg yolk

for the garnish
fresh strawberries
mint leaves

For the filling: Place all the ingredients in a bowl and mix well with a wooden spoon until everything is incorporated.

For the pastry: Place the flour in a mound on a board and make a hole in the middle of it. Put the eggs and the rest of the ingredients, apart from the single egg yolk, into the hole and work the flour in from the edges toward the centre. Knead the mixture lightly and quickly until you have a soft dough. Wrap the pastry in greaseproof paper and leave it to rest in the fridge for half an hour.

Preheat the oven to 175°C (gas mark 3). Divide the pastry into two halves. Take one half, roll it out and place it on a greased 30cm baking tin. Spread the ricotta filling over the top. Take the other piece of pastry and roll it out. With a sharp knife, cut strips about 1.5cm wide and place these over the filling, forming a criss-cross pattern. Brush the pastry with the egg yolk, put the crostata in the oven and cook it until the pastry becomes golden in colour. This should take about 25 minutes. Remove it from the oven and leave it to cool before chilling it in the fridge.

To serve, put a generous slice of the chilled crostata on each of the 4 serving plates and garnish with strawberries and a fresh mint leaf.

Wood Quay

L'Ecrivain Restaurant
SALLYANNE AND DERRY CLARKE

For as long as I can remember I have enjoyed trying new and exciting foods. That's what comes from growing up in a family of food importers. But what really sealed my fate was a summer job at The Man Friday in Kinsale under Peter Barry when I was fifteen – or should I say, four summer jobs, as I enjoyed it so much I went back there time and again. I moved to Dublin in 1977, spent four years at Le Coq Hardi and then a further eight at Bon Appetit before opening L'Ecrivain with my wife Sallyanne in July 1989. And what an incredible time we've had here, receiving many accolades for our food, wine list and service over the years, including the Bushmills Dining in Ireland awards for Best Restaurant in 1999 and 2000 and Best Chef in 2000 and 2001.

I think the reason for our success is that I believe in keeping things simple. As you can see in the recipes that follow, I never use more than four flavours in any dish, and because I feel strongly that a good dish can only be produced when each and every one of those ingredients is of the highest quality possible, I spend a lot of time sourcing our produce, using smaller, organic producers whenever I can and promoting the use of indigenous and seasonal products. The result? Contemporary Irish food at its best.

I think it'll be the depth of flavour that will surprise you most when recreating our dishes, especially if you do attempt the full menu. To taste them at their best, open a bottle of Réserve du Vigneron with the Black Pudding – a Côte du Rhone Village in which the grenache and syrah blend to produce an amazingly flavoursome concentration of fruit. Then enjoy the wonderful spice and vanilla of the Château Thieuley with the West Coast Lobster, and indulge in a glass of light, fresh Laurent Perrier Rosé with the Terrine of Summer Berries to bring out all those raspberry and strawberry flavours.

I am proud to be a part of Ireland's vibrant food culture and if you enjoy what follows, we'd be delighted to welcome you to L'Ecrivain to try some more.

L'ECRIVAIN RESTAURANT

Starter

Boudin of Clonakilty black pudding
with a Cashel blue cheese and cider sorbet,
potato mousseline and crispy bacon

Wine suggestion: Réserve du Vigneron, 2000,
Côte du Rhone Villages, Domaine Alary,
Cairanne (France)

Main course

West Coast lobster
with mango and buttermilk risotto, and
served with carrot and ginger froth and
lobster oil

Wine suggestion: Château Thieuley, 2000,
Cuvée Francis Courcelle (France)

Dessert

Terrine of summer berries
with white chocolate ice cream and
whiskey custard

Wine suggestion: Laurent Perrier Rosé (France)

Menu

Boudin of Clonakilty black pudding

with a Cashel blue cheese and cider sorbet, potato mousseline and crispy bacon

for the black pudding
1 ring of Clonakilty black pudding or
   other good quality black pudding
1 breast of chicken
1 shallot, diced
1 sprig of fresh thyme, chopped
a little salted butter
salt and freshly ground black pepper

for the Cashel blue cheese
   and cider sorbet
90g Cashel blue cheese, cut into small
   cubes
100ml cider
200ml lemon sorbet (readymade is
   fine), softened

for the potato mousseline
2 medium-sized potatoes (60g in
   total), peeled and cut into chunks
10g salted butter
1 clove of garlic, finely chopped
250ml double cream
4 sprigs of fresh thyme
salt and freshly ground white pepper

for the crispy bacon
4 rashers of streaky bacon
1 tsp vegetable oil

For the boudin of Clonakilty black pudding: Take the skin off the black pudding and crumble it into a bowl. Chop the chicken breast in a food processor until it is well broken down. Sauté the diced shallot and chopped thyme for a few minutes in a little butter over a gentle heat, and then allow them to cool. When the shallot and thyme have cooled, combine them with the black pudding and chicken and season the mixture well. Form the mixture into a sausage shape about 5cm in diameter. Roll the sausage in cling film and then in tin foil and steam or poach for 20–25 minutes. Once it has cooked, allow it to cool and then cut it into slices. Pan-fry these slices for approximately 1 minute on each side, ensuring that they are heated right through.

For the blue cheese and cider sorbet: Add the Cashel blue cheese cubes and cider to the softened sorbet, mix thoroughly and refreeze.

For the potato mousseline: Cover the potatoes with salted water, bring them to the boil and allow them to simmer for 20 minutes until soft. Drain the potatoes and mash them until smooth and fluffy. Melt the butter, add the garlic and sweat it off over a gentle heat for 2–3 minutes, making sure that it does not colour. Add the cream and thyme and let the liquid reduce by half – expect this to take about 5–10 minutes. Pass the cream mixture through a fine sieve, put it into a clean pan and return it to the heat. Gradually add the mashed potato, stirring constantly until it has the consistency of a smooth thick sauce, then season well.

For the crispy bacon: Preheat the oven to 180°C (gas mark 4). Lightly grease an oven tray with the vegetable oil and lay the bacon rashers flat on it, without allowing them to overlap. Lightly grease the underside of another oven tray of a similar size and place it on top. Bake the bacon in the oven for 8–10 minutes until it is crisp. Now remove the trays from the oven and allow the bacon to cool.

To serve, place the black pudding slices in the centre of each of the 4 serving plates and put a scoop of sorbet on top. Rest a rasher of crispy bacon in an upright position against the sorbet, put the potato mousseline into a squeezy bottle and pipe a circle of it around each plate.

West Coast lobster

with mango and buttermilk risotto and served with carrot and ginger froth and lobster oil

for the risotto
2 shallots, diced
1 clove of garlic, crushed
50g butter
200ml fish stock
100g Arborio rice
1 mango, peeled and diced
50g Parmesan cheese, grated
50ml buttermilk (or 3 tbsp crème
    fraîche)
salt and freshly ground black pepper

for the carrot and ginger froth
a little butter
2 carrots, finely diced
50g fresh ginger, peeled and finely
    diced

2 shallots, finely diced
1 tbsp white wine
90ml fish stock (readymade is fine)
90ml double cream
salt and freshly ground black pepper

for the lobster oil
shells from the lobster
3 cloves of garlic, skin on and lightly
    crushed
1 small bunch of fresh rosemary
100ml vegetable oil

for the lobster
4 x 500g live lobsters (ready-cooked
    chilled or frozen lobsters are fine)

For the risotto: Sweat the shallots and garlic in the butter for 2 minutes until the shallots are soft. Add the rice and mix well, ensuring it is coated with butter. Bring the fish stock to the boil and gradually add it to the pan, a ladleful at a time, allowing the rice to absorb all the liquid after each addition before adding any more stock. It is cooked when all the liquid is absorbed and the rice is *al dente*. Add the mango, Parmesan cheese and buttermilk (or crème fraîche), season, mix well and cook until the rice is tender. If the risotto is a little dry, add a little more buttermilk (or crème fraîche).

For the carrot and ginger froth: Sweat the carrots, ginger and shallots over a gentle heat in a little butter for a few minutes, but do not allow them to colour. Add the wine and allow it to reduce until there is very little of it left. Add the fish stock and simmer until a syrupy consistency is reached. Add 60ml of the cream and reduce until the mixture has thickened. Liquidise in a food processor or blender and pass through a fine sieve. Season the sieved mixture, add it to the

remaining cream then, using a balloon whisk or hand blender, whisk it until it becomes frothy.

For the lobster oil: Preheat the oven to 150°C (gas mark 2). Using a rolling pin, break up the lobster shells and place the pieces on a roasting tray. Add the garlic and rosemary and bake in the warm oven for about 20 minutes, until the shells are dry and lightly coloured. Place the shells, along with the garlic and rosemary, into a heavy-based pot, add the oil and leave the pan on a low heat for 4–5 hours until the flavours have infused the oil. The oil should be a light red colour with a sweet lobster taste.

For the lobster: You could use live lobsters for this recipe, in which case bring a large pot of salted water to the boil over a high heat and, making sure the water is boiling fast to ensure the lobster is killed quickly and humanely, put one lobster into the pan and cover it. Cook for 5 minutes, remove it and leave it to cool. Reheat the water for each lobster, always making sure that the water is boiling fast before putting the next lobster into the pan. When the lobsters are cool, remove the meat from the shells.

To serve, place a small mound of the mango and buttermilk risotto in the centre of each of the 4 serving plates. Put some lobster meat on top and surround them with a drizzle of the lobster-infused oil.

Terrine of summer berries

with white chocolate ice cream and whiskey custard

for the summer berry terrine
570ml raspberry coulis or purée
    (readymade is fine)
2 tbsp water
2 leaves of gelatin, soaked in cold
    water
8 slices of white bread, crusts removed
30g blueberries
30g strawberries, hulled and halved
30g raspberries
30g blackberries

for the white chocolate ice cream
275ml whipping cream
275ml milk

1 vanilla pod, split and seeds removed
    (or 1 tsp vanilla essence)
6 egg yolks
100g caster sugar
100g white chocolate

for the whiskey custard
275ml whipping cream
275ml milk
1 vanilla pod, split and seeds removed
    (or 1 tsp vanilla essence)
40ml whiskey
6 egg yolks
100g caster sugar

For the summer berry terrine: Line a loaf tin with a double layer of cling film, ensuring that it covers every side and is wide enough to cover the top. Mix half of the coulis with the water, pour the liquid into a wide tray and soak the bread in it for 10–15 minutes in the fridge. Heat the remaining coulis in a pan, add the blueberries, cook them for 1 minute and then add the strawberries. Squeeze the water from the gelatin. Remove the pan from the heat, add the remaining berries and then add the gelatin to the warm mixture. At this stage, you could also add a little ground cinnamon or star anise. The extra spice that they give works extremely well with the fruit. Use the soaked bread to line the loaf tin evenly without any overlaps. Half-fill the lined tin with the berry mixture and put a layer of bread over the top of it. Add the remaining berry mix and cover with some more slices of bread. Bring the overhanging cling film up over the top of the tin and chill it for 1^1/$_2$ hours before serving.

For the white chocolate ice cream: Put the cream and milk into a pan, add the vanilla pod or essence and bring to the boil. (Using a vanilla pod will give a richer flavour and a nicer colour to the custard.) Whisk the egg yolks and sugar together until the mixture is pale. After the milk mixture has come to the boil, remove it from the heat and slowly add it to the egg and sugar mixture, whisking constantly. Return the mixture to the pan and place it on a low heat. Cook the mixture, stirring constantly until it coats the back a spoon. Once cooked, remove it from the heat, strain it and put it in the fridge to chill. Put the mixture in an ice-cream machine and set it to churn for 30 minutes.

Meanwhile, break up the white chocolate, put the pieces in a bowl that is sitting over a pan of hot water and allow it to melt gently. After the ice cream mixture has been churning for 20 minutes, add the melted white chocolate and then leave it to churn for the final 10 minutes. Remove the churned mixture from the ice-cream machine and freeze it for at least 45 minutes to 1 hour before serving.

For the whiskey custard: Put the cream and milk into a pan, add the vanilla pod or essence and the whiskey and bring them to the boil. Whisk the egg yolks and sugar together until the mixture is pale. After the milk mixture has come to the boil, remove it from the heat and slowly add it to the egg and sugar mixture, whisking constantly. Return the mixture to the pan and place it on a low heat. Cook the mixture, stirring constantly, until it coats the back of a spoon. Once the sauce is cooked, remove it from the heat, strain it and put it in the fridge to chill.

To serve, remove the terrine from the loaf tin and slice it into 4 pieces. Place a slice of terrine on each of the 4 serving plates with a scoop of the white chocolate ice cream and drizzle the whiskey custard around them.

Ha'penny Bridge

Ely Wine Bar & Café

SARAH ROBSON

'Whatever you do, do not go into the restaurant business.' So said my parents, owners of the restaurant above which we lived. So of course, I had to do as my parents said.

The wine bar was actually my brother's idea. Erik has a real passion for wine, and turned his dream into a reality a couple of years ago when Ely's doors opened for the first time. I got involved because he asked me to create a menu as part of the business plan. Most of my food knowledge comes from working over weekends and holidays alongside my mother (with her still saying don't go into this business!), but Erik got me to work during the opening back in December of 2000 and I'm still here today.

We try to keep the food simple, Irish and traditional wherever possible – which goes with the relaxed seating and low tables as well. We love people to come in and enjoy a glass of wine or celebrate with a bottle of champagne, and the food is there more as an accompaniment, but one that is also capable of speaking for itself.

I have chosen these dishes because they reflect the rich, no-frills style of food we create here at Ely. We try to source the ingredients locally, like the organic meats from our father's farm in Co. Clare. The salad provides a contrast of flavours that works beautifully with L'Amourier 2000 from Luc Lapeyre – a lively white aperitif made from grenache blanc, muscat and bourboulenc which has a nice depth and crisp acidity to balance the anchovies and mizithra. Together they whet the appetite for the traditional main course of Honey-baked Shank of Lamb, which I recommend with another special wine from the South of France – a Côtes du Rhône from Domaine de la Janasse called Les Garrigues, 1999, in which you can enjoy the complex aromas and flavours of its eighty-year-old vines. While full-bodied enough to complement the organic lamb, the grenache grape gives pepper and licorice on the nose, and a dry, spicy finish that is not over-powering. Pleasantly satisfied you then finish with a light, palate-cleansing Summer Fruit Compote – so why not round off your meal with a glass of Lustau sherry called Emilin, whose rich raisins and dark, luscious fruit are fantastic for pouring over your ice cream.

ELY WINE BAR AND CAFÉ

Starter

Roast smoked organic chicken breast salad
with lemon marinated anchovies, croutons
and mizithra

Wine suggestion: L'Amourier, 2000, Luc Lapeyre
(France)

Main course

Honey-roast organic shank of lamb
on a bed of creamed potatoes with
caramelised shallots and red currants

Wine suggestion: Les Garrigues, 1999, Côtes du
Rhône, Domaine de la Janasse (France)

Dessert

Summer fruit compote
with a crème fraîche and
cinnamon ice cream

Wine suggestion: Emilin, Lustau sherry

Menu

Roast smoked organic chicken breast salad

with lemon marinated anchovies, croutons and mizithra

for the anchovies
55ml extra virgin olive oil
juice of 1 lemon
160g large anchovies

for the salad dressing
50g white wine vinegar
25g whole grain mustard
10g caster sugar
1 clove of garlic, crushed
150g extra virgin olive oil

for the croutons
4 slices of stale white bread
25g extra virgin olive oil
a pinch of table salt

for the roast smoked organic chicken
a 1.6kg organic smoked chicken

for the salad
1 head of lolo rossa
1 head of oak leaf
75g rocket

for the garnish
200g fresh mizithra, grated (Parmesan
   is fine)
a selection of fresh mixed herbs

For the anchovies: The day before serving, put the oil and lemon juice into a bowl and marinate the anchovies in the mixture overnight in the fridge.

For the salad dressing: To allow the flavours to infuse, the dressing is also better made the day before. Whisk the vinegar, mustard, sugar and garlic together until the sugar is dissolved. Then slowly whisk the oil in. Pour the dressing into a screw-top jar and store it in the fridge, giving the jar a vigorous shake just before you use it.

For the croutons: Preheat the oven to 180°C (gas mark 4). The croutons can also be made in advance if they are kept in an airtight container. Cut the crusts off the bread and then cut it up into small cubes. Pour the oil into a small bowl and add the salt. Toss the bread cubes in the salted oil, put them on a baking sheet and cook them in the oven for 20 minutes. Several times during the cooking time, take the baking sheet out of the oven and give it a shake so that the cubes turn over.

For the roast chicken: Preheat the oven to 180°C (gas mark 4). Put the chicken in a roasting tin, cover it with tinfoil and cook it for 1^1/$_2$ hours. Take the chicken out of the oven, remove the tinfoil and return the uncovered chicken to the oven for a further half an hour. Allow the chicken to cool slightly and then carve the breasts and remove the brown meat from the bones.

For the salad: Wash the lettuces and rocket and thoroughly dry the leaves before using them.

To serve, place a handful of the mixed leaves in the middle of each of the 4 serving plates and put a selection of chicken meat around them. Put some grated mizithra on top and drizzle the dressing over. Scatter the croutons around the plate and finally, place the anchovies on the top and garnish with the fresh herbs.

Honey-roast organic shank of lamb

on a bed of creamed potatoes with caramelised shallots and red currants

for the honey roast lamb shanks
1 bunch of fresh oregano or thyme
8–10 medium shallots, peeled and
  halved
2 medium carrots, peeled and diced
1 tray of oyster mushrooms or button
  mushrooms, washed
4 sticks of celery, washed and diced
3 cloves of garlic, peeled and finely
  sliced
2 small trays of redcurrants
$^{1}/_{2}$ bottle red wine
$^{1}/_{2}$ small jar of set honey

4 x 400g organic lamb shanks (ask
  your butcher to cut them in half so
  that you have 8 pieces in all)
salt and freshly ground black pepper

for the creamed potatoes
1.35kg rooster potatoes, peeled and
  cut into chunks
175g salted butter
300ml double cream
salt and freshly ground black pepper

For the honey roast lamb shanks: Preheat the oven to 170°C (gas mark 3). Put 4 small sprigs of the oregano or thyme on one side for the garnish. Then put the remaining herbs, vegetables, garlic, 1 of the trays of redcurrants, the red wine and three-quarters of the honey into a casserole with a tight-fitting lid – or you can use an ovenproof dish covered with tinfoil – and mix everything together. Then put the lamb shanks on top, sprinkle them with salt and pepper, cover the dish and put it in the oven for 1–1$^{1}/_{2}$ hours (until the meat is coming away from the bone). Turn the oven up to 200°C (gas mark 6). Take the lamb shanks out of the casserole or ovenproof dish and transfer them to an oven tray. Drizzle the rest of the honey over them and put them back in the oven for a further 15–20 minutes. Check the seasoning, put them into a saucepan and keep them hot until you are ready to serve.

For the creamed potatoes: Bring the potatoes to the boil and simmer them until they are soft. Drain the potatoes and cover them with a dry clean cloth. In another pot, melt the butter, add the cream and heat them up but do not allow them to boil. Mash the potatoes until there are no lumps and then add the butter mixture and salt and pepper to taste. You might not need all the butter mixture or, depending on how floury your potatoes are, you may need a little more. So add the butter mixture gradually rather than putting it all in at once.

To serve, arrange the vegetables on the plate with some creamed potatoes on top. Then, on each plate, place two halves of a lamb shank on the potato, pour over the juices from the vegetables and garnish the dish with the rest of the redcurrants and the reserved sprigs of herb.

Summer fruit compote

with a crème fraîche and cinnamon ice cream

You can serve this compote either hot or cold, but after a rich main course like the one above, I prefer to have it cold as it has a sharper taste. If you do choose to serve the compote cold, make it either on the morning of serving or the night before and refrigerate it.

for the ice cream
2 sticks of fresh cinnamon
150g caster sugar
110ml water
4 organic egg yolks
570ml crème fraîche

for the fruit compote
raspberries
blackcurrants

blackberries
strawberries
gooseberries
cherries
100g of caster sugar
zest and juice of 1 orange
a dash of sherry

for the garnish
a handful of cherries or other fruit

For the ice cream: Place the cinnamon sticks, sugar and water in a saucepan and boil them for approximately 8–10 minutes, until the mixture becomes syrupy. (This is called stock syrup.) Leave the stock syrup to cool slightly and then remove the cinnamon sticks from it. The organic egg yolks will give your ice cream a lovely rich colour. Put them in a blender and whisk them until they are light and fluffy. Now slowly add the warm syrup, making sure the mixture remains light and fluffy. Next add the crème fraîche. You want to keep as much air as possible in the egg mixture, so fold it in slowly and gently. Pour the mixture into a container and freeze it for 15–24 hours. Alternatively, you could use individual small dishes that are lined with cling film – these will only take 8–10 hours to freeze.

For the fruit compote: Any combination of the fruits listed is fine and you will need a total weight of about 900g. Put the fruit, sugar, orange juice and sherry into a saucepan, bring it to the boil and then simmer for 10–15 minutes, stirring occasionally. The compote is now ready to serve.

To serve, place scoops of the cinnamon ice cream in the middle of the 4 serving plates, pour the compote around the edge and garnish with a few cherries.

Eustace Street

Jacob's Ladder

ADRIAN ROCHE

Straightforward and easy-going – my food reflects my approach to life. For me, being a chef allows me to be creative. It's an art form, if you like, the sauces and tastes my canvas, and I became a restaurateur to have freedom. I should have known better. My first job found me peeling vegetables in the local hotel in Dalkey, Co. Dublin. And although the place is long gone, the experience lasted in that I went on to get formally trained before working my way around Europe.

My wife Bernie and I opened Jacob's Ladder in September 1997 where seasonally inspired menus take the best of modern French and Irish cuisine and combine them in dishes which are a journey of trial and error – but with the emphasis on success!

Scallops are the king of shellfish, as far as I'm concerned, and always taste great no matter how we serve them. We chose the sautéed scallop dish for its simplicity, a marriage of three simple ingredients in which the caramel of the scallops and richness of the pea purée are lightened by the mild acidity of the orange sauce to give you the perfect start to the meal – and also a quick one, making it ideal for home entertaining. Ironstone, a Semillon Chardonnay from Western Australia, matches this dish perfectly as its slightly citrus, oaky flavour is not too heavy for the shellfish. This is followed by the robust roasted squab pigeon – the heart of the menu. Although a red meat, squab pigeon has a distinctive, full flavour that everyone should try, and this particular recipe shows how simple methods can be used to make a roasted bird that little bit special. For a wine that complements the pigeon without overpowering it, you could do a lot worse than L'Amourier, 1999, from the South of France. And for dessert, the combination of pears, Baileys and coffee make a tasty but easy finish to the meal, especially if accompanied by a glass of Muscat Vin de Glacière. Enjoy!

JACOB'S LADDER

Starter

Sautéed scallops
with pea purée and an orange
and vanilla sauce

Wine suggestion: Ironstone, 2000, Semillon
Chardonnay (Australia)

Main course

Roast breast of squab pigeon
with pigeon legs en croute and pâté

Wine suggestion: L'Amourier, 1999,
Minerois A.C., Luc Lapeyre (France)

Dessert

Iced Baileys parfait
with coffee-poached pears

Wine suggestion: Muscat Vin de Glacière, 2000,
Bonny Doon Vineyard (California)

Menu

Sautéed scallops
with pea purée and an orange and vanilla sauce

The earthy pea purée and the tangy orange and vanilla sauce make the perfect partners for these beautifully sweet and succulent sautéed scallops.

for the pea purée
1/2 small onion, finely chopped
1/2 clove of garlic, crushed and chopped
10g unsalted butter
200g peas, fresh or frozen
50ml white chicken stock
salt and freshly ground black pepper

for the orange and vanilla sauce
juice of 3 small oranges

1 vanilla pod, split
1 tsp vanilla or caster sugar
10g unsalted butter, chilled

for the scallops
12 large fresh scallops, roe removed
  (ask your fishmonger to do this)
a little oil, for sautéing

For the pea purée: Sweat the onion and garlic in the butter over a gentle heat until they become transparent but without allowing them to colour. Add the peas and chicken stock to the pan and cook rapidly until the stock has evaporated. (If you are using frozen peas reduce the amount of stock by half.) Immediately blend the mixture until smooth and pass it through a fine sieve. Season the purée to taste and either keep it warm or reserve it and reheat it later.

For the orange and vanilla sauce: Place all ingredients, except the butter, in a deep pan, bring them to the boil and cover the pan with a lid. Continue to cook for 2 minutes. Allow the sauce to cool and then strain it through a sieve. It can be made, up to this stage, a day in advance. To finish the sauce, bring it to the boil and add the butter, whisking until it has all been incorporated. Keep the sauce warm until you are ready to serve.

For the scallops: Heat a heavy frying pan and sauté the scallops in the oil at a high temperature for 30 seconds. Turn them over and sauté them on the other side for another 30 seconds.

To serve, gently reheat the pea purée. Put 3 scallops in a line down the centre of each plate. Using two tablespoons, shape the purée into small quenelles (spoon-like shapes) and place on top of each scallop. Spoon the sauce around and serve the dish immediately.

Roast breast of squab pigeon
with pigeon legs en croute and pâté

This offers a little twist on traditional roast poultry. It takes a little work but your effort will be well rewarded. Ask your butcher or poulterer to prepare the pigeon squabs for you. (Use wood-pigeons if squabs are not available.) Each pigeon needs to be jointed to give two breasts and two legs and ask for the livers as well.

for the pâté
25g unsalted butter
4 pigeon livers
1 duck or chicken liver
1 small onion, finely chopped
1 clove of garlic, crushed
1 tbsp cognac
1 tbsp port
1 tbsp single cream
salt and freshly ground black pepper

for the pigeon breasts
2 tbsp pomace olive oil
8 pigeon breasts
salt and freshly ground black pepper

for the roast carrots
2 tbsp pomace olive oil
12 baby carrots, peeled but left whole
1 sprig of fresh rosemary
salt and freshly ground black pepper

for the pigeon legs en croute
8 pigeon legs
10g unsalted butter
1 sprig of fresh thyme, finely chopped
1 stalk of celery, finely diced
1 small carrot, finely diced
1 small potato, finely diced
100ml red wine
200ml chicken stock
200g puff pastry (readymade is fine)

for the sauce
30ml port
200ml brown chicken stock
  (readymade is fine)
salt and freshly ground black pepper
10g unsalted butter

for the accompaniment
creamy mashed potatoes

For the pâté: Heat a frying pan, add the butter and gently sauté the 4 whole pigeon livers, plus the duck liver, until sealed. Add the onion and garlic and continue to cook for 1 minute, without allowing them to colour. Turn the heat up, add the cognac and port and reduce the liquid by half. Add the cream, bring it to the boil, and remove the pan from the heat. Put the mixture in a blender and purée it until it is smooth. Push the puréed mixture through a sieve, season it, wrap it in clingfilm and put it in the fridge for 20 minutes to set.

For the pigeon legs en croute: Remove the skin from the pigeon legs and dice the flesh as finely as possible, reserving the bones for later. Put the butter into a deep pan and put the pan on to a moderate heat. Add the diced leg meat and cook it for a couple of minutes, without allowing the meat to colour. Add the thyme and diced vegetables, increase the heat, add the red wine and reduce it until the pan is almost dry. Add the stock and bring it to the boil. Reduce the heat and simmer for approximately 30 minutes, until the meat is tender and the sauce has thickened. Place the mixture in the fridge. When it is cold, roll it into 4 evenly sized balls.

Preheat the oven to 200°C (gas mark 6). Roll out the pastry until it is quite thin and cut it into 4 circles of about 8cm in diameter. Place a ball of the pigeon leg meat mixture in the centre of each pastry disk and stick a leg bone in the middle of each ball, drawing the pastry up around the sides to meet at the top. Press the pastry closely round the bone, leaving part of the bone visible so that it resembles a small leg of ham. Place the pigeon legs en croute on a baking tray and bake them for 10 minutes. Remove the little pastry parcels from the oven and keep them warm.

For the roast pigeon breasts: Preheat the oven to 200°C (gas mark 6). Put a heavy-based ovenproof frying pan on to a high heat, add the oil and seal the pigeon breasts on both sides. Continue frying the breasts at a moderate temperature for about 2 minutes until they are nicely browned. Season them, transfer the pan to the oven and roast the pigeon breasts for approximately 10 minutes. They should be medium cooked and, when pressed, they should have a little give. Allow them to rest in a warm place for 4 minutes, reserving any cooking juices in the pan. Carve the pigeon breasts from the bone, place the sliced meat on an ovenproof plate and put it in the oven to keep warm.

For the roast carrots: Make sure the oven is still at 200°C (gas mark 6). Meanwhile, put all the ingredients in a roasting pan and cook them for about 10 minutes, allowing them to get a good colour – this will bring out their natural sweetness.

For the sauce: Skim off the fat from the reserved cooking juices, add the port and reduce it until it becomes syrupy. Now add the chicken stock and reduce its volume by half. Season the sauce and then whisk in the butter.

To serve, place 4 baby carrots in the middle of each of the 4 serving plates. Place the 2 pigeon breasts on top, with 1 leg en croute at 10 o'clock and a spoonful of pâté at 2 o'clock. Spoon the sauce around and present the plates with some creamy mashed potato in a separate bowl.

Iced Baileys parfait
with coffee-poached pears

Although this is quite a rich-tasting parfait, it is surprisingly light and therefore does not make a filling end to the meal. The parfait needs to be frozen overnight so you will need to make it the day before serving.

for the stock syrup
300ml water
400g granulated sugar

for the parfait
500ml stock syrup
2 egg yolks
27ml water
60g granulated sugar

90ml Baileys (or any cream liqueur)
150ml double cream, whipped

for the coffee-poached pears
150ml strong coffee
4 medium-sized pears, peeled but with
   the stalks left on

for the garnish
a few mint leaves

For the stock syrup: Bring all the ingredients to the boil and simmer until the sugar has dissolved. Allow to cool and store in the fridge until needed.

For the parfait: Put the egg yolks and 20ml of the stock syrup into a mixing bowl and use an electric whisk at high speed to combine them. Meanwhile, boil the water and sugar together to make a light brown caramel. Immediately add the caramel to the egg mixture and whisk at high speed until it has doubled in size. Stop whisking and allow the mixture to cool. Add the Baileys and fold in the whipped cream. Pour the mixture into four 75mm steel ring moulds, or a bread tin lined with cling film, and freeze overnight.

For the coffee-poached pears: Put the coffee and remaining 480ml of the stock syrup in a pan and bring the liquid to the boil. Reduce the temperature to a simmer, just below boiling point, and add the pears. Cover the pan with greaseproof paper and weigh the paper down with a lid from a smaller pot. Cook for about 20 minutes until the pears are tender. Allow the pears to cool in the syrup.

   To serve, remove the parfait from the moulds and place one in the centre of each of the 4 serving plates. Position a poached pear on top, spoon some of the poaching liquid around and garnish with some mint leaves.

Bachelor's Walk

La Mère Zou
JACQUES CARRERA

To be born in France is to be born into food. Ask any kid over there about a béchamel sauce and you'll find that most of them know what it is. I'm not saying that the French are best, simply that eating in France is a lifestyle – like stout for the Irish and soccer for the Argentineans.

If you'd asked me fifteen years ago if I wanted to become a chef, however, the answer would probably have been no. My first job was actually as an electrician, but after my National Service I decided to start all over again and at the age of twenty-three became a commis chef in a one-star Michelin establishment. Learning to cook is a lengthy process and one that takes everything out of you, but after several years working my way up through the ranks I eventually got to the top.

Eric Tydgadt's restaurant has been open since 1994 and our name actually means 'mummy Zou' which, as Eric says, encapsulates our whole philosophy. We cook traditional French country food such as Côte de Bœuf Gillée and Navarin d'Agneau Printanier. But we make a point of avoiding the fuss and flurry that so many other restaurants are prone to now, and go out of our way to ensure that every single customer feels cherished and as comfortable as if dining in their own home.

I always compare a meal to a symphony. Composed of three or four dishes, it has to be balanced and in harmony so that you don't get overly full and can enjoy each of the courses until the end without discomfort. Choosing wine can be difficult so it's always best to get a second opinion – in this case our maître d' Franck Aman. Try the starter that follows with the mellow Domaine des Quarres, 1999, because the sweet side of the wine matches the foie gras and its suave flavour works beautifully with the asparagus. For the rabbit we suggest Clos de l'Echo, 1996, an intense and spicy red made from Cabernet Franc grapes that works perfectly with game, complementing the sauce and marinade. And what better way to soothe the acidity of the strawberry tart than the sweet and spicy dessert wine Maury?

Eating is an extraordinary experience; it's not just about satisfying hunger but awakening the senses. I hope you leave the table after eating the dishes that follow with a great feeling.

LA MÈRE ZOU

Starter

Bouchon de foie gras pané
sur crème d`asperge
(Breadcrumbed foie gras
on an asparagus coulis)

Wine suggestion: Domaine des Quarres,1999,
Côteaux du Layon, Maine-et-Loire, Anjou
(France)

Main course

Fillet de lièvre
rôti au lard
(Roasted hare fillet
wrapped in bacon and with a parsnip mash)

Wine suggestion: Clos de l'Echo, 1996, Chinon,
Indre-et-Loire, Touraine (France)

Dessert

Tarte aux fraises
(Strawberry tart with vanilla ice cream)

Wine suggestion: Maury (10-year-old),
Pyrennées Orientales, Perpignan (France)

Menu

Breadcrumbed foie gras

on an asparagus coulis

Bear in mind that foie gras is expensive so read the recipe carefully and try to buy only what you need. If you have to buy it whole, cut the 400g needed for the dish and use up the leftover piece quickly. You will find fresh foie gras in gourmet shops.

for the marinade

2g sugar

5g salt

2g freshly ground black pepper

55ml cognac

55ml port

for the asparagus

1 bunch of green asparagus

a pan of boiling water

a pinch of salt

for the asparagus coulis

75g shallots, peeled and chopped

stalks from the bunch of asparagus, chopped

50g salted butter

1 sprig of fresh thyme

150ml white wine

275ml chicken stock (readymade is fine) or water

275ml pouring cream

a pinch of salt

a pinch of freshly ground black pepper

for the balsamic reduction

150ml balsamic vinegar

125g plain honey

for the foie gras

400g foie gras

6 egg yolks

425ml milk

450g plain flour

450g breadcrumbs

olive oil for deep frying

for the garnish

1 packet of edible flowers

For the marinade: If you leave the foie gras at room temperature for 30 minutes, it will soften, making it easier for you to take off the nerves inside with a knife. Mix the sugar, salt and pepper together, sprinkle the mixture all over the foie gras and put it in a bowl. Mix the cognac and port together and pour the liquid over. Cover the bowl with cling film and leave it in the fridge to marinate for 45 minutes.

For the asparagus: Trim the asparagus to roughly 9cm from the head, keeping the remainder of the stalks for the coulis. Peel the trimmed spears with a vegetable peeler, going from just under the head to the end and taking care not to remove too much. Drop the spears into boiling water, adding some salt to reactivate the boiling process. Cover and cook until under *al dente*. Plunge them straight away into icy water but do not leave them in too long or they will go soggy. You want to leave them just long enough to refresh them and keep the colour. Allow them to dry on kitchen cloth and leave them until you are almost ready to serve the dish.

For the asparagus coulis: Gently sweat the shallots and asparagus stalks in the butter for 5 minutes. Add the thyme and wine and reduce the liquid until it is nearly dry. Add the chicken stock or water and cook for 15 minutes over a medium heat. Pour in the cream and increase the heat, reducing the coulis by about one-third. Add the seasoning and blend everything together in a food processor for a few minutes. Pass the coulis through a sieve and check the seasoning. The sauce should not be too runny.

For the balsamic reduction: Mix the balsamic vinegar and honey together and put the mixture into a pan. Cook at a low temperature for 30 minutes, allowing it to reduce to a consistency that coats the back of a spoon. Remove the pan from the heat and allow the balsamic reduction to cool down in the fridge.

For the foie gras: Cut the marinated foie gras using a ring cutter with a diameter about the size of a wine cork. This should give you approximately 12 pieces. Mix the egg yolks and milk together. Dip the foie gras pieces first in the flour, shaking off any excess, then in the egg and milk mixture and, finally, in the breadcrumbs.

Timing is everything when cooking foie gras so the following instructions must be observed very carefully. If you overcook it, it will become oily and this must be avoided at all costs. You must also take into account the fact that, even when you have removed the foie gras from the deep-fat fryer, the intense heat will cause it to continue cooking. It is therefore imperative that everything is ready before you begin to fry the foie gras.

So, using the balsamic reduction, make a design of spaced black dots on each of the 4 serving plates. Ensure the deep-fat fryer is hot – set it at 180°C. Make sure the coulis is warm and the asparagus spears are reheated. Lower the cork-shaped breadcrumbed foie gras pieces into the hot oil, cooking them for no longer than 1 minute. Remove them from the fryer and pat them dry on kitchen paper. Then, working as quickly as possible, dress the plate to look like the one in the photo and present the plates at once.

Roasted hare fillet

wrapped in bacon and with a parsnip mash

This is what I would call a 'masculine' dish. It has a strong flavour and, if you prefer a milder taste, use rabbit instead of hare. Personally, I would go for the hare every time! Ask your butcher to bone the saddle keeping the skin on each side and ensuring that the sides are still joined to each other. Also, be sure to ask for the bones back to use in the sauce. You will need to allow at least six hours for the hare to marinate.

for the marinade
150ml Chinon red wine
5g caster sugar
30ml brandy
1 sprig of fresh thyme
1 sprig of fresh rosemary
a few peppercorns
2 bay leaves
1 star anise

for the sweetbread
400g veal sweetbread
cold salted water

For the marinade: Cut each of the two saddles in half across the body of the hare so that you have four joined pieces. Check that there are no small pieces of bone remaining and remove any that you find. Put the hare into a dish. Mix all the marinade ingredients together and pour the mixture over the hare. Cover the dish, place it in the fridge and allow the hare to marinate for at least 6 hours.

For the sweetbread: Soak the sweetbread in cold water for 5 hours, changing the water from time to time. By the end of the soaking time, the sweetbread should have turned white. Put the sweetbread in cold salted water and slowly bring it to the boil. After 2 minutes of boiling, remove the sweetbread and refresh it under cold running water. Remove the skin and fibres that surround the sweetbread and reserve it for later.

for the sauce
bones from the hare, chopped
1 small carrot, peeled and chopped
1 onion, peeled and chopped
55ml groundnut oil
275ml Chinon red wine
20g plain flour
2 tbsp brown sugar
75ml balsamic vinegar
100g button mushrooms, sliced

for the vegetables
4 parsnips, peeled and chopped
salted water
25g salted butter
freshly ground black pepper

2 tbsp truffle oil
4 small carrots
4 small potatoes
4 small courgettes

for the hare
4 hare pieces, cut from 2 saddles
  weighing about 900g each
salt and freshly ground black pepper
8 rashers of smoked bacon, thinly
  sliced
about 1 metre of string
olive oil, for frying

for the garnish
truffle oil

For the sauce: Preheat the oven to 240°C (gas mark 9). Put the chopped hare bones, carrot and onion in an oven tray with a little oil and roast them in the oven for 15 minutes. Drain off the fat and deglaze the tray with a little of the red wine. Put the bones and vegetables in a saucepan and sprinkle the flour on top.

Remove the hare pieces from the marinade and place them on one side. Strain the marinade, discarding the remaining ingredients. In another saucepan, melt the brown sugar at a moderate temperature until a caramel has formed. Deglaze the pan with the balsamic vinegar and add the rest of the red wine, along with the marinade liquid and the sliced mushrooms. Bring the mixture to the boil, pour it into the other saucepan – the one with the bones and vegetables in it – and bring it back up to the boil again. Skim off the fat and any impurities, simmer the sauce for 25 minutes and then strain it – it should still be quite liquid at this stage. Now put the sauce back on the stove, at a medium heat, and reduce it until the sauce has a thicker consistency. Check the seasoning and put the sauce to one side until you are ready to serve.

For the vegetables: Drop the parsnips into boiling salted water and cook them for 20 minutes. Drain the parsnips and mash them to a purée, adding the butter, pepper and a little of the truffle oil. Check the seasoning. Turn the carrots, potato and courgettes so that they are shaped like knives (see the photograph) and cook them in separate pans of salted water until they are tender. Drain them then refresh them in cold water.

For the hare: Preheat the oven to 230°C (gas mark 8). Place the hare pieces on the worktop, skin side down and with the saddle open. Look in between the two sides and you should see two little fillets, lying parallel to each other with a space in the middle about the size of a finger. Cut the sweetbread into 4 pieces of around this size and put one piece in between each of the 4 pairs of fillets. Season the hare pieces with salt and pepper and roll them lengthways to form a cylinder shape, overlapping the skin and pulling it tight. Then wrap two rashers of bacon round each cylinder and secure each one with a length of string.

Pan-fry the cylinder-shaped hare pieces in hot oil for 4 minutes, turning them frequently so that they colour evenly. Transfer the hare pieces to a roasting pan and put them in the oven for 9 minutes. Remove the hare pieces from the oven, cover them with tin foil and allow them to rest for few minutes. By this stage, you should have reheated all the vegetables and the sauce, ready to put on the plates.

To serve, put a pool of sauce over the bottom of each of the 4 serving plates. Place some parsnip mash in the middle, with the vegetables neatly arranged around it. Finally, after removing the string, cut each hare piece into three medallions, arrange them on top of the parsnip mash, add a few drops of truffle oil and serve immediately.

Strawberry tart
with vanilla ice cream

This is a really delicious way to end any meal. Make sure that the strawberries are ripe and eat the tart on the day it is made. Do not refrigerate – otherwise the pastry will go soggy.

for the sweet shortcrust pastry
3 egg yolks
85g icing sugar, sifted
175g unsalted butter, diced and at
    room temperature
250g medium strength plain flour

for the pastry cream
500ml milk
1 vanilla pod, split lengthways
30ml dark rum
6 egg yolks
100g caster sugar
25g plain flour
20g cornflour

for the strawberry coulis
110g caster sugar
100ml water
200g fresh strawberries

for the topping
250g fresh strawberries

for the accompaniments
4 scoops of good quality vanilla ice
    cream (readymade is fine)
a few mint leaves
1 punnet of redcurrants

For the sweet shortcrust pastry: In a large mixing bowl beat the egg yolks and the icing sugar together. Add the butter and incorporate the flour with your fingertips until you get a sandy dough. Do not over mix. Roll the pastry into a ball, wrap it in cling film and let it rest in the fridge for 6 hours.

Remove the pastry from the fridge and allow it to come to room temperature. Meanwhile, butter the inside of four 9cm tartlet cases. Flour the work surface and roll the dough out until it is quite thin. Leave it to rest for a few minutes before cutting it with a 13.5cm pastry cutter. Line the tartlet cases with the pastry circles, pressing the pastry firmly into the sides and trimming away any excess from round the edges. Now put the tartlet cases in the fridge to rest for a further 10 minutes.

Preheat the oven to 190°C (gas mark 5). The tartlets need to be baked blind to stop the bases rising and prevent the sides from collapsing. To do this, line the pastry cases with baking parchment and fill them with ceramic baking beans (dried beans will work just as well). Bake the pastry cases in the oven for 10 minutes. Take them out, remove the beans and the baking parchment and then bake them again for 2 more minutes. Remove the pastry cases from the oven and put them in a dry place.

For the pastry cream: In a saucepan, bring the milk to the boil. Add the vanilla pod and the rum, reduce the heat and simmer slowly for 5 minutes so that the vanilla infuses. Take the pan off the heat and remove the vanilla pod.

Put the eggs yolk and sugar into a bowl, beat them together and then whisk in the flour and the cornflour. Pour half of the hot milk on to the egg mixture to dissolve everything. Put the egg mixture into a pan and bring the mixture to the boil, whisking all the time until smooth. Then add the remaining milk and cook again for another 2 minutes, still whisking. Take the pan off the heat and allow the mixture to cool down before putting it in the fridge.

For the strawberry coulis: In a saucepan, combine the caster sugar with the water, bring the mixture to the boil and let it simmer for 3 minutes. Allow the syrup to cool down and then add the strawberries and blitz in a blender for a couple of seconds. Pass the coulis through a sieve and put it in the fridge until you are ready to serve the tartlets.

To serve, spoon the pastry cream into the tartlet cases until they are three-quarters full. Slice the strawberries and arrange them so that they slightly overlap one another and form a circle on top of the pastry cream. (If you want to glaze the tarts, you could buy some readymade jelly but I prefer to leave them unglazed as this allows the full taste of the strawberries to come through.) Put a small pool of coulis on each serving plate and place a tartlet on it. Now top each tartlet with a scoop of ice cream and decorate with a mint leaf and a small bunch of redcurrants.

O CONNELL

Daniel O'Connell Monument, O'Connell Street

Moe's Restaurant

IAN CONNOLLY AND ELAINE MURPHY

Food allows your creativity to flourish. It also allows you to be yourself – the two things that most attracted me to becoming a chef. Not to mention Mum's cooking, of course! I started at Moe's in June 2000, having worked at the Balmoral in Edinburgh and all over my home town of Dublin. We go out of our way to create a casual, comfortable ambience here so that our customers can sit back and relax into the combinations and textures for which our modern Irish menu is famed.

The vegetarian menu I have selected for this book demonstrates this beautifully. The textural contrasts and distinctive flavours in the starter, for instance – the herb-flavoured tomatoes, rich goat's cheese mousse, tangy pickled onions and crunchy rocket salad – are balanced by the softer, richer main course focused around the Parmesan potato cakes with mushrooms and crème fraîche. And for a memorable finish to any meal, the coconut tart – a personal favourite of mine! – is a must, especially if you enhance the tropical feel with pineapple syrup and rum and raisin ice cream.

MOE'S RESTAURANT

Starter

Rocket and marinated plum tomato salad
with goat's cheese mousse, pickled red
onions and olive tapenade

Wine suggestion: Bonny Doon Solo, 2000,
Malvasia Bianca, Monterey (California)

Main course

Parmesan potato cake
with oyster mushrooms, sautéed spinach,
chive crème fraîche and truffle oil

Wine suggestion: Cortes de Cima Chaminé,
1999, Alentejo (Portugal)

Dessert

Coconut tart
with rum and raisin ice cream and
pineapple syrup

Wine suggestion: Essensia Orange Muscat,
1998, Andrew Quady (California)

Menu

Rocket and marinated plum tomato salad

with goat's cheese mousse, pickled red onions and olive tapenade

for the plum tomatoes
2 sprigs of fresh rosemary
2 sprigs of fresh thyme
$1/2$ a clove of garlic, finely sliced
100ml extra virgin olive oil
10 plum tomatoes, skinned, sliced and
  deseeded

for the goat's cheese mousse
50g mature goat's cheese
50ml double cream, whipped

for the pickled red onions
$1/2$ red chilli
1 star anise
125g caster sugar
$1/2$ tsp salt
275ml water

175ml red wine vinegar
3 medium red onions, sliced into fine
  rings

for the black olive tapenade
100g black olives
1 shallot
25g fresh basil
25g fresh flat-leaf parsley
$1/2$ a clove of garlic
100ml extra virgin olive oil

for the rocket salad
2 tbsp olive oil
a squeeze of lemon juice
salt and freshly ground black pepper
4 handfuls of rocket

For the plum tomatoes: Put the rosemary, thyme, garlic and olive oil in a bowl with the tomatoes and marinate them in the fridge for 1 hour. Strain the marinade through a sieve, reserving the liquid to use as a dressing. Place the plum tomatoes on one side, picking out the garlic and herbs.

For the goat's cheese mousse: Put the goat's cheese in a blender and whizz it until it is smooth. Place it in a bowl and fold in the whipped cream.

For the pickled red onions: Put all the ingredients except the sliced onions into a pan and bring them to the boil. Add the onions, take the pan off the heat and allow the mixture to cool. Leave the onions pickling until you are ready to serve the dish.

For the black olive tapenade: Put all the ingredients except the olive oil in a blender and, while blending, gradually add the olive oil.

For the rocket salad: Mix the olive oil, lemon juice and seasoning together and toss the rocket in the mixture.

To serve, neatly cover the bottom and side of a 75cl cutter with the marinated plum tomatoes. Almost fill the rest of the cutter with mousse, and top it with the remainder of the tomato slices to form a neat circle (see the photograph). Put the cutter in the centre of a bowl or plate and place 3 onion rings evenly around the edge, spooning some of the tapenade in between. Remove the pastry cutter and place some rocket salad neatly on top of the tomatoes, spooning the marinade oil around the edge of the dish to finish.

Parmesan potato cake

with oyster mushrooms, sautéed spinach, chive crème fraîche
and truffle oil

for the Parmesan potato cake
700g plain mashed potato (the rooster
  variety works well for this)
100g Parmesan cheese, thinly shaved
50ml extra virgin olive oil
salt and freshly ground black pepper
100g Parmesan, finely grated
300g brioche breadcrumbs (normal
  breadcrumbs are fine)
150ml milk
2 eggs
100g plain flour

for the oyster mushrooms
4 large shallots, finely sliced

1 tsp garlic purée
a little butter and oil, for frying
100g oyster mushrooms
salt and freshly ground black pepper

for the spinach
4 handfuls of spinach, washed
a little butter
a little cold water
salt and freshly ground black pepper

for the garnish
4 tbsp crème fraîche
1 bunch of fresh chives, finely chopped
4 tbsp white truffle oil

For the Parmesan potato cake: Put the Parmesan shavings in the hot mashed
potato. Add the olive oil, salt and pepper and mix thoroughly. Divide the mash
evenly into 4 and shape it with a 75cl pastry cutter. Cover the 4 potato cakes and
place them in the fridge for 1 hour. Mix the finely grated Parmesan with the
breadcrumbs, and whisk the milk and eggs together. Coat the potato cakes in
flour, then dip them in the milk and egg mixture and, finally, coat them in the
Parmesan and breadcrumb mixture, ensuring that they are completely covered.
Leave the potato cakes to set in the fridge for another hour.

   Preheat the oven to 190°C (gas mark 5). Shallow- or deep-fry the potato cakes
until they turn golden brown and then place them on a baking tray in the oven
for 5 minutes or until heated through.

For the oyster mushrooms: Fry the shallots and garlic in the butter and oil over a
high heat for 30 seconds. Turn the temperature down to moderate, add the oyster
mushrooms and continue frying for a few minutes until the mushrooms are just
cooked. Add salt and pepper to taste.

For the spinach: Cook the spinach in a hot pan with the butter, a little water and the salt and pepper for 30 seconds.

To serve, put some of the mushroom and shallot mixture in the centre of each of the 4 serving plates. Place the spinach on top of this and then top the spinach with a Parmesan potato cake. Spoon one tablespoon of crème fraîche over each one and sprinkle the chives on top. Lastly, drizzle the truffle oil around the plate.

Coconut tart

with rum and raisin ice cream and pineapple syrup

If you are making your own ice cream, you will need to prepare it the day before serving.

for the rum and raisin ice cream
100g raisins
100ml dark rum
12 egg yolks
250g caster sugar
600ml milk
600ml cream

for the coconut tart filling
2 whole eggs
3 egg yolks
200g caster sugar
250g creamed coconut

300ml coconut coulis (or unsweetened
    coconut milk)
300ml double cream

for the pastry
65g unsalted butter
65g icing sugar
1 egg, beaten
155g plain flour

for the pineapple syrup
500ml water
1 baby pineapple, finely diced
250g caster sugar

For the rum and raisin ice cream: Soak the raisins in the rum for at least 24 hours. Beat the egg yolks and caster sugar together until they are white and creamy. Put the milk and cream into a pan and bring them to the boil. Add the hot milk and cream to the egg and sugar mixture and combine them. Return the mixture to the pan and cook it on a very low heat, constantly stirring, until it coats the back of a spoon. Allow it to cool and then add the rum-soaked raisins. Churn the mixture in an ice-cream machine and then leave it in the freezer overnight.

For the coconut tart filling: Beat the eggs, egg yolks and sugar together and then add the creamed coconut. Mix the coconut coulis (or coconut milk) and cream together, add them to the egg and sugar mixture and mix everything thoroughly.

For the pastry: Cream the butter and icing sugar together and slowly add the beaten egg. Mix in the flour, cover with cling film and allow the mixture to rest in the fridge for 1 hour.

Preheat the oven to 170°C (gas mark 3). Roll the pastry out as thinly as possible and use it to line an 18cm tart tin. Cover the pastry base with baking parchment and fill it with ceramic baking beans (dried beans or pasta shapes will work just as well). The beans will stop the pastry base rising and will also prevent the sides from collapsing. Bake the pastry case for 10 minutes, then take it out of the oven and remove the beans and parchment. Now add the coconut filling and return the tart to the oven for a further 30 minutes. When ready, remove the tart from the oven and leave it to cool.

For the pineapple syrup: Put all the ingredients in a pan and bring them to the boil. Simmer until the pineapple is tender.

To serve, place a wedge of tart on each of the 4 serving plates. Put a scoop of rum and raisin ice cream next to it and drizzle the pineapple syrup around the edge of the plate.

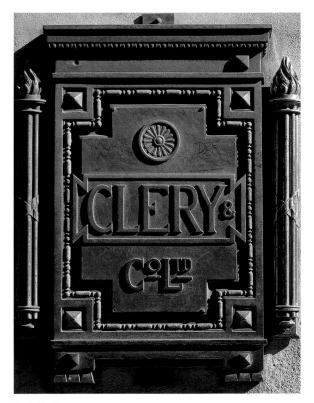

Sackville Place

O'Connells in Ballsbridge
RORY AND TOM O'CONNELL

It should be said that I fell into the cookery business by default. I have had no formal training, but initially began working in the kitchens at Ballymaloe House Hotel in Co. Cork just for fun. To my great surprise, I discovered that I loved cooking and wasn't too bad at it either! After working in many top restaurants, I returned to Ballymaloe in 1995 as Head Chef, and am the founding partner of the Ballymaloe Cookery School. I visit O'Connells regularly, working with our Executive Chef, Felix Zund, and Head Chef, Brian McCarthy.

My brother Tom's route to O'Connells came through a career in hotel management. On graduating from SCoHM in 1976, he spent exactly twenty years abroad with Hilton International in New York, Brussels, Gatwick and London, then at The Savoy and The Ritz in London. He finally came back to Ireland to manage The Berkeley Court Hotel in Dublin, and did not hesitate to join me in creating and managing O'Connells in Ballsbridge when it opened in 1999.

Our style is modern Irish – embellishing traditional food with a little modern and international flavour and zest. The ingredients in my three dishes are very special and work well together for several reasons. The smoked fish comes from a smokehouse in Cobh in East Cork where they are traditionally produced to the highest standard. Frank Hederman who produces the fish is one of the best in the country and we are proud to use his produce. The pickled cucumbers help to cut through this flavoursome smoked fish, whilst the duck to follow creates a real contrast. We like to spit-roast our ducks whole in the traditional manner, as this gives the authentic flavour we like. The accompanying spiced nectarines and buttered courgettes add taste and visual interest – the nectarines add a little sweetness, whilst the courgettes help to balance the richness of the duck meat. The shortcake is full of rich flavours and textures and is a classic and simple expression of the best quality ingredients . . . Irish butter and flour in the shortcake, and rich Irish cream with succulent strawberries in the topping. A heavenly way to end the meal.

Tom (left) and Rory O'Connell

O' CONNELLS IN BALLSBRIDGE

Starter

Plate of Frank Hederman's smoked fish with chive mayonnaise and pickled cucumber

Wine suggestion: Pinot Blanc d'Alsace, 2000, Cave de Turckheim, Alsace (France) – available from James Nicholson, Crossgar, Co. Down

Main course

Duck roast with spiced nectarines and buttered courgettes

Wine suggestion: Tulbagh Merlot, 2000, Paarl, Cape Town (South Africa) – available from The Wine Vault, Waterford

Dessert

Strawberry shortcake

Wine suggestion: Muscat de Beaumes de Venise, Delas Frères (South of France) – available from Febvre & Co., Dublin

Menu

Plate of Frank Hederman's smoked fish
with chive mayonnaise and pickled cucumber

If you can't get hold of Frank's marvellous produce, use the best fish from your own part of the world.

for the chive mayonnaise
4 tbsp mayonnaise (readymade is fine)
2 tbsp fresh chives, chopped

for the pickled cucumber
1 small cucumber, very finely sliced
1 small onion, very finely sliced
110ml white wine vinegar
150g caster sugar
a pinch of salt

for the smoked fish
4 slices of smoked salmon

4 x 25g pieces of smoked mackerel
8 smoked mussels
4 x 15g pieces of smoked eel
4 smoked sprats

for the garnish
4 wedges of lemon
4 sprigs of fennel

for the accompaniments
brown crusty bread
Irish butter

For the chive mayonnaise: Mix the chives into the mayonnaise.

For the pickled cucumber: Mix all the ingredients together and leave them to macerate for at least 1 hour. If you put this pickle in a screw-top jar, it will keep for a week in the fridge.

To serve, divide the smoked fish evenly between 4 large white serving plates, arranging the seafood to make the most of the different colours and textures. Place a neat little mound of pickled cucumber on each plate, along with a wedge of lemon and a sprig of fennel, and present the fish with the brown crusty bread and delicious Irish butter.

Duck roast

with spiced nectarines and buttered courgettes

We like to spit-roast duck in the traditional way as this makes the meat very tender and gives it a lovely old-fashioned flavour. However, for this recipe more conventional methods taste just as good.

for the spiced nectarines
1/2 red or green chilli, split and
   deseeded
1x 3cm piece of fresh ginger, peeled
4 cloves
110ml white wine vinegar
275ml water
225g caster sugar
4 ripe nectarines

for the duck
a 1.5kg free-range duck
sea salt and freshly ground black
   pepper

275ml duck or chicken stock
   (readymade is fine)
50g salted butter
a squeeze of lemon juice

for the buttered courgettes
10g salted butter
15ml olive oil
225g courgettes, cut into 3mm slices
sea salt and freshly ground black
   pepper

for the garnish
4 sprigs of flat-leaf parsley

For the spiced nectarines: Put all the ingredients, except the nectarines, into a stainless steel saucepan, bring everything to the boil and cook for 1 minute. Quarter the nectarines, remove the stones and add the pieces to the pan. Simmer the fruit gently until it is just tender. Allow the mixture to cool and reserve 8 tablespoons of the liquor for deglazing the roasting tin. Cover the remainder and store it in the fridge until you are ready to dish up.

For the roast duck: Preheat the oven to 200°C (gas mark 6). Season the skin and cavity of the duck with the salt and pepper and place it in a roasting tin. Put the duck in the oven and roast it for 1 1/2 hours until it is cooked through. Remove it from the oven and put it on a hot plate, reserving the fat. Lower the oven temperature to 50°C and return the duck to the oven to rest.

Drain the fat from the roasting tin and place the tin on the stove on a moderate heat. Add the reserved nectarine liquid, allow it to come to the boil and add the stock, scraping the bottom of the tin with a whisk to free any stuck-on caramelised juices. Continue to cook the sauce until these juices have dissolved into the liquid. Strain the sauce into a small saucepan and put it on a moderate heat. Reduce the liquid until it becomes syrupy. Add the butter and swirl it into the sauce. Taste to check the seasoning and add some lemon juice if you think it needs it.

For the buttered courgettes: Only begin to cook the courgettes when you are just about ready to serve the duck. They don't take long and overcooking them will result in them becoming limp and dull. Heat the butter and oil in a non-stick pan over a medium heat. Add the courgette slices, season them and fry them until they are barely tender, tossing the pan to ensure they are cooked on both sides.

To serve, carve the duck, ensuring that there is some leg and breast meat for each portion. Put some buttered courgettes on each of the 4 warmed serving plates and arrange some duck meat on top of them. Space 4 quarters of spiced nectarine round each plate, drizzle some sauce over the duck and garnish the plates with a sprig of parsley.

Strawberry shortcake

This simple dish never fails to please. However, we only serve it when the native strawberries, with their distinctive flavour, are in season.

for the shortcake biscuits
175g plain (cream) flour
110g unsalted butter
50g caster sugar

for the garnish
a little icing sugar
4 sprigs of fresh mint

for the strawberry topping
12 ripe Irish strawberries (or fresh
   locally grown ones)
275ml whipping cream, whipped

For the shortcake biscuit: Preheat the oven to 190°C (gas mark 5). Put the flour into a mixing bowl and rub the butter into it using the tips of your fingers until the mixture resembles fine breadcrumbs. Add the sugar and work it in so that it comes together to form a dough. Don't be tempted to add water to bind the dough at this stage – just keep kneading the mixture and it will form a dough on its own. Roll this out on a floured worktop until it is about 3mm thick. Cut out 8 biscuits using a biscuit cutter of the shape of your choice. Put the biscuits on a baking tray and bake them in the oven for about 10 minutes until they are golden brown. Remove the tray from the oven and carefully transfer the biscuits to a wire rack to cool.

For the strawberry topping: Keeping 4 strawberries whole and un-hulled, hull the other 8 and carefully slice them from top to bottom.

   To serve, place a shortcake biscuit on each of 4 large white serving plates. Carefully fan some strawberry slices on top of each one and put a generous blob of whipped cream on top of them. Place another biscuit on top to form a lid, then position an un-hulled strawberry on top of this biscuit, dust the plates with icing sugar and garnish them with the sprigs of mint.

Ormond Quay Lower

Pearl Brasserie
SEBASTIEN MASI AND KIRSTEN BATT

I believe it was my early and unsuccessful exit from school in France that contributed to the start of my apprenticeship, at the age of fifteen, in a small country house. Here we worked on an old wood cooker, making our own cured ham, fishing for lunch in the river and picking mushrooms, rhubarb and apples from the garden.

Hungry to push further, at the age of seventeen I took my knife and went to Paris, where I began working in the newly-opened Copthorne Hotel. It was a really organised place, with three restaurants and twenty-five chefs. The quality and quantity of produce were amazing – ten different types of mushroom, white truffles, caviar by the kilo and a profusion of foie gras, lobster . . . The wages were small, but so were the hours, which gave me the opportunity to work on a casual basis in many of the other kitchens in the city, such as the Meridien Etoile and Hotel Intercontinental St Claire, and outside catering with M. Guy Savoie (three-star Michelin) and M. Gerard Besson (two-star Michelin). It was good to see the differences in styles of cooking and organisation – from thirty covers to 800, and from traditional to modern cuisine.

It was only in 1994 that, with my ten words of broken English, I arrived in Dublin. I spent my first year working at the two-star Michelin Restaurant Patrick Guilbaud, before gaining my first position as head chef in Commons Restaurant – one of the most elegant eighteenth-century town houses in Dublin and an example of Ireland's Georgian heritage.

But the idea of opening my own restaurant would not go away, so, with the help of my partner, Kirsten Batt, Pearl Brasserie was born on 7 December 2000. Our philosophy is simple – good food and comfortable surroundings, with friendly and attentive staff. We serve traditional French cuisine in a warm, modern, informal environment, with jazz playing in the Oyster Bar as you relax beside a giant peat fire and exotic aquarium.

I have chosen the dishes that follow because they epitomise the best in lazy summer dining, all the ingredients – strawberries, rhubarb, pears – being in season between June and September. But they also take you on a culinary journey around France while giving you the true taste of Pearl. Happy cooking!

149

PEARL BRASSERIE

Starter

Pan-fried duck foie gras
with rhubarb and strawberry compote on
toasted brioche

Wine suggestion: Les Aunis, 1994, Côteaux du
Layon Chaume, Château de la Roulerie, Anjou
(France)

Main course

Blue lobster
with sautéed potatoes flambéed in
Irish whiskey

Wine suggestion: Frog's Leap Chardonnay, 1999,
Napa Valley (California)

Dessert

Chocolate and pear mousse
rolled in crushed mixed nuts

Wine suggestion: Royal Tokaji Aszu Five Puttonyos,
1996, Royal Tokaji Wine Company (Hungary)

Pan-fried duck foie gras
with rhubarb and strawberry compote on toasted brioche

for the rhubarb and strawberry
   compote
200g rhubarb, washed and chopped
   into pieces about 4–5cm long
100g caster sugar
8 strawberries, washed and diced

for the foie gras
4 x 120g slices of duck foie gras
salt and freshly ground black pepper

for the accompaniment
4 large slices of toasted brioche
2 figs, halved

For the rhubarb and strawberry compote: Put the rhubarb and sugar into a pan and cook it gently until it is softened. (There is no need to add any water when cooking rhubarb.) When it is cooked, leave it to drain, then mix it with the diced strawberries while the rhubarb is still warm.

For the foie gras: Season the slices of foie gras with the salt and pepper on both sides. Heat up a large pan without adding any oil. Place the seasoned foie gras in the heated pan and cook it for just 30 seconds on each side.

To serve, put a slice of toasted brioche on each of the 4 serving plates, spread some rhubarb and strawberry compote over them and place the slices of pan-fried foie gras on top, garnishing with half a fig.

Blue lobster
with sautéed potatoes flambéed in Irish whiskey

4 blue lobsters, live

for the sautéed potatoes
400g potatoes, peeled, cut into chunks
   and boiled
2 dsp olive oil
salt and freshly ground black pepper

6 large shallots, peeled and sliced
4 cloves of garlic, peeled and crushed
40g salted butter
a pinch of fresh parsley, chopped
150ml Irish whiskey
fresh dill, to garnish

For the blue lobsters: Bring a large pan of salted water to the boil and cook the lobsters for 3 minutes. Cool them down under cold running tap water, then cut each of the tails into 5 cylinder shapes, ensuring that the shells remain attached. Break down the claws and take the flesh out.

For the sautéed potatoes: Try to get the ratte variety of potatoes – they have a lovely nutty flavour. Slice the boiled potatoes, put them in the olive oil in a non-stick pan and pan-fry them over a moderately high heat. Season and, once they reach a nice golden colour, add the shallots, garlic and pieces of lobster. Toss all the ingredients together for 1 minute and then add the butter and chopped parsley. Add the whiskey and light it, being careful with the flame.

   To serve, put everything into a large serving dish, garnish with the dill and breathe in all the delicious smells. Place the serving dish in the centre of the table so that your guests can dig in and help themselves.

Chocolate and pear mousse
rolled in crushed mixed nuts

This quantity serves six so put the two spare mousses in the fridge to enjoy the next day!

for the crushed mixed nuts
10g pistachio nuts
10g hazelnuts, peeled
10g almonds
10g pecan nuts
10g icing sugar

for the chocolate and pear mousse
200g caster sugar
275ml water
2 pears, peeled and diced

200ml crème anglaise (readymade is fine)
100g bitter dark chocolate, at least 70% cocoa solids
1 leaf of gelatin, soaked in cold water for 5 minutes
200ml whipping cream, whipped

for the accompaniment
4 scoops of good quality ice cream

For the crushed mixed nuts: Preheat the oven to 180°C (gas mark 4). Put all the nuts on a roasting tray and dust them with the icing sugar. Roast the nuts in the oven for 10 minutes, take them out and, when cooled, roughly crush them together using a rolling pin.

For the chocolate and pear mousse: Put the sugar and water into a pan and boil them vigorously for 5 minutes. Reduce the heat to moderate, add the diced pears and simmer them for a few minutes until they are tender. In a bowl sitting over a pan of hot water, warm the crème anglaise and melt the chocolate. Squeeze the water out of the gelatin and, once the chocolate has melted, add the gelatin to the bowl and mix everything together. Allow the mixture to cool down by placing the bowl over some ice. Drain the pears, add them to the bowl and mix. Now incorporate the whipped cream into the mixture. Pour the mixture into 6 ramekins and place them in the fridge for 2 hours to set. Slightly warm the bottom of the ramekins over some boiling water, turn them upside down and gently allow the mousses to slide out. Now delicately roll them in the prepared mixed nuts.

To serve, place one chocolate and pear mousse on each of the 4 serving plates and present with a generous scoop of vanilla ice cream.

O'Connell Bridge

Shanahan's on the Green
LEO SMALL

Cooking is my life. I am passionate about it and I enjoy the hard work. Being brought up in a catering family meant that my fate was sealed from an early age. But although I worked in the evenings and at weekends in my father's butchers shop, and in the local fish and chip shop during the summer holidays, I didn't really get bitten by the chef bug until I had a part-time job working in a local restaurant as a kitchen porter. When the chef was busy, he would call on me to help peel the potatoes and prepare the vegetables. When he could see I had an interest in cooking, he asked me to work on the line. I agreed because anything was better than washing dishes, so I guess it all started there!

Shanahan's is an American-style steakhouse with an emphasis on beef. Our menu maintains a seasonal appeal and not only features locally grown produce and seafood but we import products as well to ensure that quality always comes first. I'd like to thank all the management, floor staff and kitchen team for their endless dedication and hard work, and a very special thanks to the Shanahan family for opening this unique restaurant.

The combination of flavours in the tuna starter are superb. The crisp salad, married with the peppery crust on the rare tuna, work very well together, while the pickled ginger, orange and cucumber not only cleanse your palate in preparation for the steak that follows but are incredibly refreshing and light to eat. A citrus riesling like the Grosset Polish Hill Riesling, 2000, is just the thing to complement the rosy tuna and stand up to all those punchy flavours, while the peach and grapefruit of Viogner, 1999, are rich and bold enough to shine through the spices. The beef at Shanahan's is certified Irish Angus. After seasoning, we broil our steaks at a very high temperature to sear the outside but keep the inside juicy and tender. The celeriac mash and caramelised onions which accompany the steak ensure that the dish is not too heavy, especially if you sip a quietly elegant wine like Il Circo, 2000, with it. Alternatively, go for the big, intense flavours of Nuits St Georges, 1998, whose silky tannins and long, long finish make it almost as perfectly balanced as a wine can be. The fragrant coconut pudding is a refreshing way to finish your meal, especially if eaten with a sweet, tropical wine like the Austrian Kracker, 1999, or Hungarian Grand Cuvée Tokaji, 1996.

SHANAHAN'S ON THE GREEN

Starter

Carpaccio of yellow fin tuna
with a beetroot, orange and sprout salad,
mushroom and soy dressing and wasabi
crème fraîche

Wine suggestions: Grosset, Polish Hill Riesling,
2000, Clare Valley (Australia) or Viogner, 1999,
Alban Vineyards, California (USA)

Main course

Shanahan's dry-rubbed rib steak
with celeriac mash and caramelised onions

Wine suggestions: Nuits St Georges, 1èr Cru,
1998, Close des Porrets, Henri F. Gouges
(France) or Il Circo, 'La Violetta', 2000, Bonny
Doon Vineyard, California (USA)

Dessert

Coconut pudding
with caramelised banana, poached
pineapple and mango sorbet

Wine suggestions: Kracher, 1999,
Trockenbeerenauslese (Austria) or Grand Cuvée
Tokaji, 1996, Oremus, Five Puttonyos (Hungary)

Menu

Carpaccio of yellow fin tuna

with a beetroot, orange and sprout salad, mushroom and soy dressing and wasabi crème fraîche

for the curry oil
125ml onion, chopped
$^1/_2$ bulb of fennel, chopped
125ml dried apricots, chopped
250ml olive oil
2 tbsp curry powder
a pinch of salt, to taste

for the mushroom and soy
   vinaigrette
250ml olive oil
2 portobello mushrooms, chopped
60ml balsamic vinegar
60ml soy sauce
freshly ground black pepper

for the wasabi crème fraîche
1 tsp wasabi paste
3 tbsp crème fraîche
1 tbsp mayonnaise (readymade is fine)
1 tbsp lime juice
salt, to taste

for the pepper crust
500g Sichuan peppercorns
300g coriander seeds
200g Maldon sea salt

for the garlic flakes (optional)
250ml whole milk
2 cloves of garlic, finely sliced

vegetable oil for deep frying
salt

for the salad
1 medium red or green chilli, cut in
   half lengthways and seeds removed
1 bunch of green scallions
a pinch of Hijiki Japanese seaweed
   (optional)
2 sticks of celery
$^1/_2$ cucumber, peeled and cut in half
   lengthways
2 large oranges
500g bean sprouts
500g salad machè or lamb leaves
25g fresh coriander leaves
25g fresh basil leaves
25g pickled ginger
8 tbsp fresh orange juice
4 tsp olive oil
20 garlic flakes (optional)

for the tuna
250g yellow fin tuna, centre cut (ask
   your fishmonger to trim it into a
   cylinder shape)
1 tbsp olive oil

for the garnish
125g braised baby beetroots, cut into
   quarters

For the curry oil: On a medium heat, sauté the onion, fennel and apricot in 2 tablespoons of the olive oil for 5 minutes or until translucent. Add the curry powder and cook for a further 3 minutes. Add the remaining olive oil and salt and simmer for another 5 minutes. Set the mixture aside for 3 hours to allow the oil to separate from the pulp at the bottom of the pan. Strain the oil through a muslin cloth or cheesecloth, pour it into a screw-top jar and store it in the fridge until you are ready to serve the dish.

For the portobello mushroom and soy vinaigrette: Heat up a medium sized sauté pan over a moderate heat and drizzle 1 tablespoon of the olive oil in the centre of it. Add the mushrooms and cook them until they are soft. Add the balsamic vinegar and the soy sauce and heat until everything has warmed through but do not allow it to boil. Remove the pan from the heat and allow the flavours to marinate for 10 minutes. Pour the vinaigrette into a medium bowl and whisk it while gradually adding the remainder of the olive oil. Pass the dressing through a fine sieve and add freshly milled black pepper to taste.

For the wasabi crème fraîche: Place all ingredients in a bowl and whisk them together until the mixture is smooth. Pour it into an airtight container and store it in the fridge until you are ready to serve the dish.

For the pepper crust: Place all ingredients in a coffee grinder and blitz them until they are powdered. Put the mixture into a fine sieve and sieve it, pushing through any lumps to powder them.

For the garlic flakes: Soak the garlic slices in the milk for 1 minute, drain them off then deep fry them in hot oil at 180°C until they are crisp. Sprinkle with salt and leave them on one side until required.

For the beetroot, orange and bean sprout salad: Cut the chilli halves into very fine strips and put them in a bowl of iced water. This will make the chilli strips curl. Cut the green part of the scallions into fine strips and put them into the iced water. If using seaweed, soak it for 10 minutes in tepid water to soften it. Using a potato peeler, peel the celery into long strips and put them in the iced water as well. Using a teaspoon, remove the seeds from the cucumber, then cut the halves into long strips about 0.5cm wide and chop the strips up so that you have diced pieces. To segment the oranges, cut a thin slice off the top and bottom of each one so that you have flat surfaces – this will prevent the oranges from rolling around. Gently peel the oranges with a sharp knife, following the curved shape of the fruit. Continue this around each orange until they are completely peeled. Now, using a sharp knife, cut quarters of orange segment from the orange between the white central parts.

Take 4 medium-sized bowls and add equal amounts of bean sprouts, machè leaves, chilli, scallion and celery to each one. Then add 3 orange segments, some of the coriander and basil leaves, a couple of pieces of the pickled ginger and a few garlic flakes (if required) to each and toss everything together. Add 2 tablespoons of the orange juice and 4 teaspoons of the olive oil and combine everything well. If using seaweed, add it at this stage.

For the yellow fin tuna: Roll the tuna in the pepper crust mixture until it is lightly coated. To help the tuna keep its shape, tightly wrap the coated fish in cling film, then leave it in the fridge for 1 hour to firm it and make it easier to sear. Once ready, remove the cling film and heat up a pan that is large enough to fit the whole tuna loin. Drizzle in the olive oil, add the tuna and sear it on all sides for 30 seconds over a medium heat. (If you would prefer the tuna a little more cooked, sear it for up to a minute. Tuna is, however, best eaten rare.) Allow the tuna to cool slightly and again tightly wrap it in cling film. This will help it to hold its shape when you slice it. Cut the tuna into 12 thin slices, which will give you 3 slices per portion.

To serve, put 5 dots of the wasabi crème fraîche around the edge of each serving plate. Place a piece of pickled ginger between them and put small leaves of coriander and basil between each piece of ginger and wasabi dot. Place 3 pieces of the quartered braised beetroot in the centre of each plate, with the salad mixture on top to form a kind of haystack. Arrange 3 slices of the seared tuna around the salad and finish by drizzling each plate with curry oil and mushroom and soy vinaigrette.

Shanahan's dry-aged ribeye
with caramelised onions and celeriac mash

for the steak jus

4 tbsp olive oil

4 shallots, roughly chopped

1 carrot, roughly chopped

2 large onions, roughly chopped

1 leek, roughly chopped

1 sprig of fresh thyme

1 sprig of fresh rosemary

1 bulb of garlic, roughly chopped

500g beef trimmings

2 tbsp balsamic vinegar

4 tbsp red wine

4 tbsp passata or tomato juice

1 litre veal stock (readymade, with the
   addition of a few fresh herbs, is fine)

1 litre beef stock (readymade, with the
   addition of a few fresh herbs, is fine)

2 tbsp soy sauce

2 tbsp Worcestershire sauce

for the Shanahan's dry rub

50g dried oregano

25g dried marjoram

$1/2$ tsp paprika

$1/2$ tsp coriander seeds

25g onion powder

25g garlic granules

25g freshly ground black pepper

100g Maldon sea salt

For the steak jus: Put the olive oil into a medium-sized pan over a high heat and sauté the shallots, carrots, onions, leeks, herbs, garlic and beef trimmings until they are a golden brown colour. Add the vinegar, wine and passata and reduce the liquid until it is almost dry. Add the veal and beef stocks, bring everything to the boil and remove any scum that forms on the surface. Keep simmering and reduce the liquid by half. Add the soy and Worcestershire sauces, taste the jus and adjust the seasoning if necessary. Pass the jus through a sieve, return it to a clean pot and reduce it until it is of a consistency to coat the back of a spoon.

For the Shanahan's dry rub: Place all the ingredients in a food processor and blitz them until they resemble fine sand. (If Maldon sea salt is not available, use rock salt but reduce the amount by half, as rock salt is saltier than Maldon.)

for the caramelised onions
2 tbsp water
15 onions, finely chopped
25ml soy sauce
25ml Worcestershire sauce
55ml steak jus
55ml Harvey's Bristol Cream
$^1/_2$ tbsp Shanahan's dry rub
50g salted butter, diced

for the mashed potatoes
8 rooster potatoes, peeled and cut into
   quarters
50g salt

for the celeriac purée
1 tbsp olive oil
50g salted butter
250g celeriac, peeled and cut into
   chunks
4 medium-sized shallots, peeled and
   chopped

the white part of 1 leek, washed and
   chopped
150ml vegetable stock (readymade is
   fine)
100ml double cream
salt and freshly ground white pepper

for the celeriac whipped potatoes
50g salted butter, diced
100ml double cream
100ml milk
about 800g mashed potato
about 500g celeriac purée
freshly ground white pepper

for the rib-eye steak
4 x 600g rib-eye steaks (see below)
Shanahan's dry rub

for the garnish
1 sprig each of fresh thyme, rosemary,
   oregano, sage

For the caramelised onions: For this, you will need a heavy-based pot that is large enough to hold all the chopped onions. Heat the water in the pan over a high heat and add the onions – the water will prevent the onions burning. When the onions start to break down and become transparent and soft, turn the heat down to medium. Mix the soy sauce, Worcestershire sauce, steak jus and Harvey's Bristol Cream together. Gradually add this liquid to the onions, allowing the moisture to evaporate. This will take time so do not rush it. When the onions start to take on a caramelised colour and you have used about three-quarters of the liquid, add the Shanahan's dry rub. Stir the pan occasionally to prevent the onions sticking to the bottom. Gradually add the rest of the liquid until is it all used up. Add the diced butter, piece by piece, and, when it has all melted, the onions should have a dark brown colour.

Remove the pan from the heat and spread the caramelised onions out on a flat baking tray to allow them to cool slightly before serving. (If you have any caramelised onions left, they are great spread on beef sandwiches with fresh horseradish.)

For the mashed potatoes: Put the potatoes and salt into a medium-sized pan of water, bring them to the boil, reduce the heat and simmer for about 20 minutes, until they are tender. Drain the potatoes and mash them. For an even smoother consistency, push the mashed potato through a sieve. While the potatoes are still warm, wrap them in cling film and store them in the fridge until you are almost ready to dish up.

For the celeriac purée: Heat the olive oil and butter in a frying pan and sauté the celeriac, shallots and leek over a medium heat for a few minutes. Add the stock and cream to the pan and continue to cook for another 10 minutes, until the vegetables are soft. Put the contents of the pan into a food processor and blitz the mixture until it is smooth. Add the salt and pepper.

For the celeriac whipped potatoes: Put the butter, cream and milk into a medium-sized saucepan and bring it to the boil. Remove the cling film from the mashed potato, add it to the pan and beat the mixture until it becomes smooth and creamy. Now add the celeriac purée, mix well and add white pepper to taste. The texture should be firm and not at all runny.

For the rib-eye steaks: The best thing to do is to ask your butcher to trim the rib roast, weighing about 3kg, of all the fat and bone so that you are left with the centre eye of the rib. Then ask him to cut this evenly into four 600g steaks and get him to tie these tightly around the outside with string to help them keep their shape while cooking. Preheat the grill at its highest setting for 20 minutes before you start cooking the steaks. At the same time as you start heating the grill, take the steaks out of the fridge, cover them with cling film and allow them to reach room temperature. Doing this will improve their flavour and release their natural juices. Lightly sprinkle the steaks with some Shanahan's dry rub, put them on a wire rack under the grill and cook them on each side until they turn golden brown. The time this takes depends on how you and your guests like steaks cooked, the following being a rough guide to total cooking times:

- medium–rare, 12 minutes
- medium, 15 minutes
- medium–well-done, 20–25 minutes

In addition, allow 3 minutes resting time after the steaks have been cooked.

To serve, warm the 4 serving plates and place a rib-eye steak in the centre of each one. Spoon some celeriac mash on to one side and a generous spoonful of caramelised onion next to this. Pour 2 tablespoons of steak jus over the steak and garnish the plates with the fresh herbs.

Coconut pudding
with caramelised banana, poached pineapple and mango sorbet

for the stock syrup
270g caster sugar
200ml water
a squeeze of fresh lemon juice

for the pineapple chips
1 pineapple
270ml stock syrup

for the coconut pudding
85g unsalted butter
100g icing sugar
25g ground almonds
85g desiccated coconut
15g cornflour
85ml egg whites
10g runny honey

for the poached pineapple
150g caster sugar
1 vanilla pod
2 cinnamon sticks
4 cloves
400ml warm water
juice of 1 lemon
1 pineapple

for the mango sorbet
100g caster sugar
50ml fresh lime juice, strained
500ml mango purée (available at good
    supermarkets)
100ml liquid glucose

for the passion fruit sauce
250ml passion fruit purée (available at
    good supermarkets)
100g caster sugar

for the caramelised banana
3 bananas
2 vanilla pods, split in half
zest and juice of 2 limes
50g caster sugar
30g unsalted butter
35ml Malibu

for the garnish
4 sprigs of fresh mint

For the stock syrup: Put the water, sugar and lemon juice in a pan, and allow them to boil for about 10 minutes until the sugar has dissolved.

For the pineapple chips: Peel and core the pineapple, cut it in half lengthways, then slice it finely and dip the slices in the stock syrup. Preheat the oven to 90°C. Shake off any excess syrup from the pineapple slices, place them on a baking tray lined with baking parchment and dry them in the oven for about 8 hours until they turn golden brown.

For the coconut pudding: Put a heavy-based saucepan on the stove to heat for 2 minutes. Add the butter and allow it to melt and turn golden brown. Set the melted butter aside and let it to cool. Place all the dry ingredients in a mixing bowl, mix them together then slowly add the egg whites. Mix the honey and cooled melted butter together and gradually incorporate the mixture into the rest of the ingredients. Preheat the oven to 160°C (gas mark 2.5). Grease 4 tian moulds

and line them with baking parchment. Pour the mixture into the moulds so that it comes to about 1cm from the top and bake them in the oven for 15 minutes. Take them out, remove the moulds by running a sharp knife round the insides and leave the puddings to cool on a wire rack.

For the poached pineapple: Put the sugar, vanilla pod, cinnamon and cloves into a heavy-based saucepan over a medium heat. Keep stirring the contents of the pan until the sugar turns light golden brown. Add the water and lemon juice and continue to heat, stirring continuously, until the caramel has dissolved completely. Peel, slice, core and cube the pineapple, add the pieces to the pan and bring them to the boil. Switch off the heat and leave the poached pineapple to cool in the syrup.

For the passion fruit sauce: Put all the ingredients into a saucepan, bring them to the boil, skim off any residue on the surface and then lower the heat. Continue to cook the mixture over a moderate heat until the volume has reduced by about half and then pass it through a sieve.

For the mango sorbet: Put the passion fruit purée and sugar into a saucepan and bring them to the boil. Allow them to cook at about 70°C for 8–10 minutes. Put the sorbet into the fridge until it is cool, churn it in an ice-cream machine and then put it into the freezer until you are ready to serve.

For the caramelised bananas: Peel the bananas and cut them into slices about 1$\frac{1}{2}$cm thick. Make a hole through the centre of each piece with a wooden skewer and thread 5 of them on each half of the 2 vanilla pods. Marinate the bananas in the zest and juice of the limes in the fridge until needed. Heat the butter and sugar in a medium-sized frying pan until they turn golden brown. Carefully add the bananas, turning them so that they are caramelised on all sides. Remove them again and deglaze the pan with the Malibu and the lime juice that the bananas were marinated in.

To serve, gently warm the coconut puddings in the oven. Place 5 pieces of poached pineapple in the centre of each of the 4 large serving plates and put a coconut pudding on top of them. Spoon 1 tablespoon of passion fruit sauce over each pudding and then put a scoop of mango sorbet on top. Carefully place some pineapple chips on top of the sorbet, along with a sprig of mint. Finally, arrange the caramelised banana pieces around the outside of each plate.

James Joyce Monument, Earl Street

Four Courts, Inns Quay

The Tea Room
The Clarence Hotel
ANTONY ELY

When your mother works at top hotels like Claridges, The Ritz and The Berkeley in London and then comes home with brilliant stories of all the goings-on there, it's pretty likely you'll end up with at least a passing interest in food. Which is exactly what happened to me. I used to love helping her out at home in the kitchen and once got a chance to cook the Sunday lunch – or rather put the meat into the oven to await my parents' return. To their complete surprise, however, I managed to put the whole meal together, minus the gravy, before they got back.

My formal training began with two years of City and Guilds, followed by fifteen years at the school of hard work, intrigue and perfection – most recently as sous chef at The Square Restaurant in Mayfair for five years. I became Executive Chef at The Tea Rooms in April 2000. Here the spacious restaurant with its high ceiling creates an airy, relaxing environment in which to enjoy our seasonal menu. And you'll find in the pages that follow three recipes that reflect the range of modern Irish dishes that we prepare – all of which are very popular with our customers and which, when eaten one after another, make a meal to remember.

You start with the juicy quail – we've managed to source Irish quail, which have a great depth of flavour – and this is accompanied by crisp potato, a sweet and tangy chutney made from in-season peaches, and a relatively new product for me, the spicy morcilla which is a bit like black pudding. Volnay Les Carelles, 1995, a velvety smooth pinot noir, is a great wine to try with this. Then on to the moist and meaty halibut, with flavour-packed gnocci, earthy mushrooms and a smooth sweetcorn sauce, not to mention a glass or two of a dry fruity wine like Clos Mireille, 1999. And finally, light and creamy yoghurt contrasting the cold sharpness of a cherry granita, all served up with warm cherries and custard in a crumbly pastry case that simply melts away in your mouth. Sip on a classic Muscat, and you've got the perfect summer dessert. Delicious!

THE TEA ROOM
THE CLARENCE HOTEL

Starter

Roast quail
with peach chutney, rösti potato and
morcilla

Wine suggestion: Volnay Les Carelles, 1er Cru,
1995, Camille Giraud (France)

Main course

Caramelised halibut
with Parmesan and herb gnocchi,
mousserons and sweetcorn velouté

Wine suggestion: Clos Mireille, 1999, Blanc de
Blancs, Domaines Ott (France)

Dessert

Vanilla yoghurt and cherry granita
with a warm cherry and custard tartlet

Wine suggestion: Muscat de Beaumes-de-
Venise, 1999, Domaine de Durban (France)

Menu

Roast quail

with peach chutney, rösti potato and morcilla

for the peach chutney
¹/₂ small onion, finely
   chopped
40g tomatoes, skinned
   and chopped
¹/₂ apple, peeled, cored
   and chopped
1 clove of garlic, finely
   chopped
¹/₂ tsp fresh ginger,
   peeled and grated
zest and juice of ¹/₂ lime
60g caster sugar
¹/₂ tsp salt
¹/₂ cinnamon stick
¹/₂ tsp grated nutmeg
30ml white wine vinegar

40g golden raisins
250g fresh peaches,
   washed, stoned and
   chopped

for the rösti potato
¹/₂ tsp salt
1 large baking potato,
   peeled
50g clarified butter (or
   olive oil)

for the quail
4 whole quails
salt and freshly ground
   black pepper
a little vegetable oil

a knob or two of butter
   for roasting

for the
   accompaniments
12 slices of morcilla
   (black pudding is also
   fine)
a little vegetable oil for
   frying
¹/₂ packet of fresh
   chives, finely chopped
1 head of frisée lettuce,
   picked
salt and freshly ground
   black pepper

For the chutney: Put all the ingredients, except the peaches, into a heavy saucepan and bring them to the boil. Simmer until the volume has reduced by one-third and add the peaches. Now reduce the mixture until it is thick and syrupy – expect this stage to take about 25 minutes. Remove the cinnamon stick and set the chutney aside until you are ready to serve.

For the rösti potato: Preheat the oven to 150°C (gas mark 2). Grate the potato or use a mandolin to shred it into strips and sprinkle it with the salt. After 15 minutes, place the salted potato shreds into a clean cloth and wring out the water. Warm the butter, mix it with the potato shreds, and place this on to a baking tray, spreading it out thinly. Using a round cutter, shape the mixture into 8 rounds. Now bake the rösti for 12 minutes, rotating the tray halfway through the cooking time. When the rösti are crisp and golden, remove them from the baking tray and place them on a wire rack to cool.

For the quail: Preheat the oven to 180°C (gas mark 4). Season the quail with the salt and pepper. Put a frying pan over a high heat with the vegetable oil and cook the birds until they are golden in colour. Transfer them to a roasting tin, add the butter and roast them in the oven for 4^1/$_2$ minutes. Allow the quail to rest and cool for a few minutes.

For the accompaniments: Pan fry the morcilla or black pudding slices in the vegetable oil over a high heat for approximately 45 seconds on each side and remove them from the pan.

To serve, place one rösti in the centre of each of the 4 serving plates. Put 3 slices of morcilla or black pudding on top of each and cover them with frisée and chives. Place another rösti on top of this and finish with a quenelle of chutney. Remove the quail legs and breast, season them and arrange two breasts and two legs around the edge.

Caramelised halibut

with Parmesan and herb gnocchi, mousserons and sweetcorn velouté

for the gnocchi
400g baking potatoes (200g when
    cooked)
1 egg, beaten
70g strong flour
35g Parmesan cheese, grated
1 packet of fresh parsley, finely
    chopped
1 packet of fresh chives, finely
    chopped
1 packet of fresh chervil, finely
    chopped
salt and freshly ground black pepper
a little vegetable oil for frying

for the sweetcorn velouté
$1/2$ onion, finely chopped
25g butter
1 clove of garlic, crushed
200g sweetcorn (fresh or frozen)
1 sprig of fresh thyme
200ml water
100ml milk
salt and freshly ground black pepper

for the mousserons
40g unsalted butter
200g mousserons or wild mushrooms,
    left whole
1 clove of garlic, lightly crushed
2 sprigs of fresh thyme

for the accompaniments
12 button onions, peeled
a little vegetable oil
100g unsalted butter
8 cloves of garlic, skins left on
a pinch of salt
1 packet of spinach, washed
20ml olive oil
salt and freshly ground black pepper

for the halibut
a little vegetable oil for frying
4 x 175g halibut steaks

For the gnocchi: Preheat the oven to 175°C (gas mark 3–4). Bake the potatoes for 1 hour, allow them to cool a little, then remove the skins. Put the warm potato and all the other ingredients, except for the oil, into a bowl and mix thoroughly. Roll the mixture on a floured board, form it into a sausage shape about 2cm in diameter and slice this at 2.5cm intervals. (These quantities will give you about 12 gnocchi.) Poach the gnocchi in salted water until they rise. Then remove them from the poaching pan and plunge them into iced water. When they are cool, take them out of the water and dry them on some kitchen paper. Fry the gnocchi in the oil over a moderate heat until they are golden, remove them from the oil and keep them warm until you are ready to serve.

For the sweetcorn velouté: Sweat the onion in half of the butter over a moderate heat for about 2 minutes until it is soft. Add the garlic, sweetcorn, thyme and water and continue to cook until the liquid has reduced to about 50ml. Put the mixture in a blender and whizz everything together. Return the mixture to the pan, add the milk, seasoning and the rest of the butter and mix well. Keep the velouté warm and give it a good whisk before serving.

For the mousserons: Put a frying pan on to a high heat and add the butter. Once it has melted, add the rest of the ingredients and simmer until the mushrooms are soft. Remove them from the pan and keep them warm until you are ready to serve.

For the accompaniments: In a frying pan, colour the button onions in a little vegetable oil. Add 30g of the butter, season and fry them gently for about 6 minutes until they are soft. Place the garlic in a small pan with the remaining butter and a pinch of salt and cook it gently over a moderate heat until it is golden. Sauté the spinach in the olive oil, season and drain.

For the halibut: Preheat the oven to 180°C (gas mark 4). Put a frying pan on to a high heat and add a thin layer of vegetable oil. Place the halibut steaks in the pan and fry them for 3 minutes on one side, allowing them to colour. Now transfer them to a roasting pan and cook them in the oven for $2^1/_2$ minutes until they are cooked through.

To serve, place some spinach in the middle of each serving plate. Put 3 gnocchi around the edge, each with a button mushroom on top, and spoon the mousserons in between. Put the halibut steaks on top of the spinach, top this with two cloves of garlic, and spoon the whisked sweetcorn velouté over the accompaniments.

Vanilla yoghurt and cherry granita

with a warm cherry and custard tartlet

The yoghurt needs to be started a day or two in advance of serving, and the granita has to be made the day before.

for the vanilla yoghurt
325ml whipping cream
125ml milk
125g caster sugar
1 vanilla pod, split
1 tsp live yoghurt culture (available in
    health food shops)

for the granita
125g cherry purée (readymade is fine)
juice of 1 lemon
125ml water
20ml Kirsch

for the custard
250ml milk
60g caster sugar
1 vanilla pod, split
3 egg yolks
20g custard powder

for the pastry
250g soft plain flour
125g unsalted butter
125g caster sugar
1 whole egg

for finishing the tartlets
24 cherries, stoned
a little icing sugar for dusting

For the vanilla yoghurt: Place all ingredients, except the yoghurt culture, into a pan. Warm them to 42°C, whisking all the time, then remove them from the heat, add the culture, whisk again and remove the vanilla pod. Pour the yoghurt mixture into glasses and put them somewhere warm (at a temperature of 42°C) for 6–7 hours until set. Now refrigerate them until needed.

For the cherry granita: Mix all ingredients together, pour the mixture into a shallow tray and freeze it. Every 15 minutes, break up the ice that forms with a fork so that you have crystals. Once the mixture is nice and flaky, place it in a chilled tub and refreeze it.

For the vanilla custard: Put the milk, half the sugar and the vanilla pod in a pan and bring it to the boil. In a clean bowl, mix the egg yolks, the rest of the sugar and the custard powder together. Pour the hot milk mixture over, stirring to avoid lumps forming, and return it to the heat. Whisk the custard until it thickens.

For the pastry: Put the flour, butter and sugar in a bowl and, using your fingertips, rub them together until they resemble breadcrumbs. Add the egg, mix until it becomes firm, cover with clingfilm and refrigerate. Preheat the oven to 180°C (gas mark 4). Roll out the pastry on a floured board to a thickness of about $^1/_2$cm and, using a 8cm pastry cutter, cut out 4 circles for the bases of the tartlets. Using a smaller cutter, cut out another 4 circles which will form the lids. Line 4 small tartlet cases with the pastry, fill them with custard, add 6 cherries to each one and cover them with the pastry lids. Place the tartlets on a baking tray and bake them in the oven for about 20 minutes. Remove them and sprinkle them with sugar.

To serve, take the yoghurt glasses out of the fridge, top them with a scoop of cherry granita and serve them with the warm cherry tartlets.

Anglesea Street

Appendices

Ormond Quay Lower

Weights, measures and servings

All weights, measures and servings are approximate conversions.

SOLID WEIGHT CONVERSIONS

Metric	Imperial
10g	$^1/_2$ oz
20g	$^3/_4$ oz
25g	1 oz
40g	$1^1/_2$ oz
50g	2 oz
60g	$2^1/_2$ oz
75g	3 oz
110g	4oz
125g	$4^1/_2$ oz
150g	5 oz
175g	6 oz
200g	7 oz
225g	8 oz
250g	9 oz
275g	10 oz
350g	12 oz
450g	1 lb
700g	$1^1/_2$ lb
900g	2 lb
1.35 kg	3 lb

STANDARDS SOLID

1 oz	=	25g
1 lb	=	16 oz
1 g	=	0.35 oz
1 kg	=	2.2 lb

LIQUID CONVERSIONS

Metric	Imperial
55ml	2 fl.oz
75ml	3 fl.oz
150ml	5 fl.oz ($^1/_4$ pint)
275ml	$^1/_2$ pint
425ml	$^3/_4$ pint
570ml	1 pint
725ml	$1^1/_2$ pints
1 litre	$1^3/_4$ pints
1.2 litre	2 pints
1.5 litre	$2^1/_2$ pints
2.25 litre	4 pints

STANDARDS LIQUID

1tsp	=	5ml
1 tbsp	=	15ml
1 fl.oz	=	30ml
1 pint	=	20 fl.oz
1 litre	=	35 fl.oz

OVEN TEMPERATURE CONVERSIONS

°C	Gas	°F
140	1	275
150	2	300
170	3	325
180	4	350
190	5	375
200	6	400
220	7	425
230	8	450
240	9	475

Contributor details

Avoca Café
11–13 Suffolk Street
Dublin 2
00 353 1 672 6019

Cavistons Seafood Restaurant
59 Glasthule Road
Sandycove
Co. Dublin
00 353 1 280 9245

Chapter One
18–19 Parnell Square
Dublin 1
00 353 1 873 2266

China Sichuan Restaurant
4 Lower Kilmacud Road
Stillorgan
Co. Dublin
00 353 1 288 4817

Dunne & Crescenzi
14 South Frederick Street
Dublin 2
00 353 1 677 3815

L'Ecrivain Restaurant
109a Lower Baggot Street
Dublin 2
00 353 1 661 1919

Ely Wine Bar and Café
22 Ely Place
Dublin 2
00 353 1 676 8986

Jacob's Ladder
4 Nassau Street
Dublin 2
00 353 1 670 3865

La Mère Zou
22 St Stephen's Green
Dublin 2
00 353 1 661 6669

Moe's Restaurant
112 Lower Baggot Street
Dublin 2
00 353 1 676 7610

O'Connells in Ballsbridge
at Bewley's Hotel
Merrion Road
Ballsbridge
Dublin 4
00 353 1 647 3304

Pearl Brasserie
20 Merrion Street Upper
Dublin 2
00 353 1 661 3572

Shanahan's on the Green
119 St Stephen's Green
Dublin 2
00 353 1 407 0939

The Tea Room
The Clarence Hotel
6–8 Wellington Quay
Dublin 2
00 353 1 676 8995

Index of recipes